DANGEROUS MEMORIES

House Churches and Our American Story

**Bernard J. Lee
Michael A. Cowan**

Sheed & Ward

Sheed & Ward™ is a service of National Catholic Reporter Publishing, Inc.

Library of Congress Catalog Card Number: 86-62123

ISBN: 0-934134-70-7

Published by: Sheed & Ward
                115 E. Armour Blvd. P.O. Box 419492
                Kansas City, MO 64141-6492

To order, call: 800-333-7373

Contents

There are dangerous memories, memories which make demands on us. There are memories in which earlier experiences break through to the centre-point of our lives and reveal new and dangerous insights for the present. They illuminate for a few moments and with a harsh and steady light the questionable nature of things we have apparently come to terms with, and show up the banality of our supposed 'realism'. They break through the canon of the prevailing structures of plausibility and have certain subversive features. Such memories are like dangerous and incalculable visitations from the past. They are memories that we have to take into account, memories, as it were, with a future content.

—Johann Baptist Metz
Faith In History And Society

PREFACE

Dangerous Memories is fundamentally an effort in practical theology. As such, it urges small communities of faith into serious and mutually critical conversation between the Christian tradition and the concerns of our time. Such conversation moves from a disciplined social and cultural analysis of the contemporary situation, to an equally careful reading of relevant aspects of our religious tradition, and then back and forth between the two. In genuinely mutual conversation neither partner seeks to control the outcome; something is put at risk for both. Like all authentic conversation, practical theological reflection within small communities will give rise to possible futures for those communities in the form of invitation and confrontation. It is these concrete alternatives for the future arising out of genuine dialogue to which small communities of faith must then say "Yes" or "No."

Both of us writing this book have some experience of house church communities in the United States. We have felt the transformative power which can arise within small, intentional Christian communities. We have lived with the strains and risks inherent in this form of life. As we watch the texture of church life in the Roman Catholic and other Christian traditions in this country undergo structural change, the emergence of a significant house church movement appears to us as a real and hopeful possibility.

We personally feel a sense of urgency in refusing to be trapped in the legendary pursuit of lonely individualism so characteristic of U.S. society. When that same individualism is raised to the level of foreign policy, it is as destructive for citizens of the world as its national version is for citizens of this country. We also recognize our own fear that the relational commitments which community requires will threaten the freedom we have come to cherish as U.S. citizens. We know that we are not alone in our double-edged response to the possibility of participation in an intentional Christian community.

The two elements contained in our subtitle, *House Churches and Our American Story,* locate more specifically the particular social phenomenon which we want to describe. "House churches" or intentional Christian communities are small groups of persons sharing a commitment in their own time and place to the ancient practices of *koinonia, diakonia, leitourgia* and *kerygma.* By "our American story" we mean the world of this text's authors and of the reading public to which it is primarily addressed, the culture of middle-class citizens of the United States of America. It is important to note that the U.S. version of "our American story" is but one aspect, albeit for better and for worse a hugely important one, of the larger story of the American continent.

We have tried here to evoke and nurture a possibility which is already emerging in the society and culture of the United States, even as it has in many other places throughout the world. The house church, or intentional Christian community, has begun to reconstruct the ecclesial life of Christians in the United States. It is, finally, both an ancient and a new way of being church. It is a way whose time is our time. We offer it for your consideration, expecting that you will sense its danger and trusting that it will likewise reveal to you its liberating hope. We have lived and continue to live with both of these responses to the world of possibility in front of our text.

The fabric of *Dangerous Memories* is, like the conversation between the authors from whence it emerged over the past ten years, largely composed of strands drawn from theology, philosophy and the social and behavioral sciences. Its weaving was an exercise in full partnership.

Bernard J. Lee
Michael A. Cowan

Chapter 1

A REGATHERING
OF THE CHURCHES

An Earthquake Phenomenon

Earthquakes reshape the foundations of the world upon which our human constructions rest. They are part of the shifts the earth must make to keep its energies and counter-energies in balance.

Something with earthquake potential has been rumbling through the Roman Catholic world for a generation now. Some dangerous things are being remembered: that all baptized women and men are responsible for the life of the Christian community; that all social structures—intimate ones and immense ones, civil ones and ecclesial ones—are put under requirement by the Gospel; that the world truly can be reconstructed into the People of God; that the reconstructions are glorious after the pain, doubt, fear and struggle, but not during the remaking. These are dangerous memories, and they are shaking some foundations.

These memories and their retrieval have to do with how followers of Jesus Christ are choosing to regather themselves to-

1

gether to minister both to their own needs and to the shifting energies and counter-energies of a world in the throes of transformation. These regathering Christians are committed to having that transformation bear the marks of the faith narrative out of which they live. With Paul Tillich, not to mention Paul of Tarsus, they believe that community is the structure of grace in human history. The role of community in the social reconstruction of the world is one of the most important sacraments of redemption, which comes from God for us but through us. In St. Louis, Boston, San Antonio, and Santa Fe, these gatherings re-instance an upper room in Jerusalem, and many other rooms, upper and lower, in Antioch, Ephesus, Corinth, Rome, etc.

What are these regathering groups like? They are small groups of Christians who gather regularly. They pray, sing, and share their human stories. They bring their stories and The Story into serious dialogue. The members know one another personally. They offer support to one another. Together they often confront the injustices of their world. With other groups, they form a network of communities. For the most part, they are grass-roots groups. No one told them to gather; they bring themselves together. They are, therefore, non- hierarchical. But the fact that their originating impetus does not come from hierarchical organization does not mean they are anti-institution. Rather, they are choosing to take care of needs (e.g., a more deeply interpersonal community) and convictions of faith (e.g., that God's reign in history requires changing unjust structures) that the institution is not addressing adequately. They do not think of themselves as extra-ecclesial, but as genuine church, as basic ecclesial units.

In Latin America these groups are called *communidades de base*, or basic Christian communities (BCCs). In Africa they are more often called small Christian communities (SCCs). Sometimes these two expressions are used interchangeably when talking about the Asian church, or about parts of the first-world church. In this book we will often use the sociological description, "intentional Christian communities" (ICCs), for such gatherings are not random. They are the result of deliberate, "intentional" choices which link these particular people to one another.

We will sometimes also use a description from the early centuries of Christian life, since these intentional communities are not a brand new movement. The house church (sometimes called "household of faith") is the normal expression of Christian community life from Paul's time through most of the fourth century. Contemporary ecclesiology asks whether the intentional communities which were "normal" in the early church should not also be *normative* basic ecclesial units in any age. (The Rite of Christian Initiation for Adults seems to presuppose their existence.)

As old as the roots of this movement are, the "regathering" movement in our times is barely a generation old. No remembered tradition can be simply repeated in another age. The contemporary movement brings the deeper instinct of the early movement to life again in new circumstances, and for new as well as old reasons.[1] But old or new, they call the settled order into question and demand more People of God configuration for the world. They put history under requirement in quite pointed ways. Archbishop Ivo Lorscheiter, speaking of the Brazilian experience, said that "from the view of church and society, the existence of the Basic Christian Communities is the most important event of our epoch."[2] It is too early to render a seasoned historical judgment, but Lorscheiter may indeed be right. A lot is afoot in many parts of the world.

When a movement rumbles into life as quickly as the ICC movement and spreads across the earth with such surprising vigor, we can be sure that it is a complicated movement whose causal impulses are multiple and varied. Especially when a movement is cross-cultural, it must be touching some raw nerves deep in the corporate psyche. To try to understand the intentional Christian community movement, we will consider shifts in metaphor and imagination stemming from the Second Vatican Council that are altering religious sensibilities in the

Western psyche. We will note a burgeoning agenda that appears
to be owned by more and more of the peoples of the world. In the
final parts of this chapter we will glance at the house church
movement in the early church, and see why these small groups,
then and now, are truly units of church.

A Shift in Metaphor

In his novel *The Unbearable Lightness of Being*, Milan
Kundera says that metaphors contain in a nutshell a basic
human possibility, and that metaphors are not to be trifled with
in view of things to which they can give birth, even to love.[3]
Kundera is reflecting upon how a novelist hits upon some
metaphor that then roots the rest of the narrative. Once the root
metaphor is grasped, the story begins to spin itself out. Paul
Ricoeur has suggested that human thought begins in metaphor.
Metaphors are not ornamental embellishments of a rational understanding. Rather, a metaphor, clothed with feeling, is the fundamental way in which we grab hold of experience. Philosophies
and theologies express the logic of the metaphor, and not the
reverse.

The Second Vatican Council gave Catholic Christians a new
root metaphor for themselves: You are the People of God. This
metaphor indeed is not to be trifled with in view of things to
which it can give birth, even to love. The ICCs are one part of
the ecclesial narrative that this new root metaphor's "logic" is
provoking. A little history will help us understand the importance of the People of God metaphor.

Anyone who studies theology in our era will almost certainly
attend to ecclesiology as one of the major disciplines. We
presume that ecclesiology, the theology of the church, is a standard piece of the theological synthesis. Surprisingly, however,
until the 16th century, ecclesiology is not a standard kind of
theological treatise. In his *Summa Theologica*, St. Thomas
Aquinas does not have a tract on the church; he moves immediately from Christ to the Sacraments.

It is in response to the Reformation that Roman Catholics begin to defend a particular understanding of the church. The expression "counter-Reformation" explains a lot: when ecclesiology does emerge as a theological discipline, it is somewhat defensive and reactive in character. I do not mean "defensive" as a negative psychological attitude; a church under attack understandably defends itself. This ecclesiology is a theology of the universal church. It does not concern itself with the particular character of particular churches, but with the "nature" of church which must characterize every particular church. In his very influential book, *Models of the Church*, Avery Dulles traces the centrality of "institution" to the church's self-understanding. At some deep level of self-perception, "institution" functions as root metaphor for the Catholic church beginning with the counter-Reformation, and a narrative structure begins to unravel out of it.

Vatican II is unique in the history of church councils. It is not called to combat a danger or to address a specific crisis. Pope John XXIII convokes the council to update the church's life (*aggiornamento*) in profound conversation with the contemporary world. In his convocation of the council, John says that "humanity is on the edge of a new era," and he wants to bring this gestating world "into contact with the vivifying and perennial energies of the Gospel."

In this atmosphere of affection for history instead of defensiveness towards it, *Lumen Gentium*, the dogmatic constitution on the church, redescribes the church. None of the notions is brand new, but the way they are weighted and inter-related is indeed quite a different story from the ecclesiology of Trent or Vatican I. The opening chapter of *Lumen Gentium* is more like a poem than a theological treatise. Biblical images, one after another, tumble forth. The second chapter proposes the biblical image of "People of God" as a central motif for the church's self-understanding. This is a finely nuanced presentation which addresses the inter-relation between hierarchical and non-hierarchical identities, yet always starts with the presumption that all people are together the one People of God. Chapter three then goes on to address the church's hierarchical realities. However, we seldom attend to all the nuances of our public documents. Our inclination is to live out of the bold-stroked picture, the metaphor, which the document evokes.[4] Placing People of God before Hierarchy is a bold stroke. Vatican spokespersons complain these days that people seem to have read the chapter on the People of God and then stopped before the chapter on Hierarchy. I think, rather, that God's people are vigorously exploring the structural implications of placing the one model before the other (though that language might not be part of their conscious awareness).

In Apostolicam Actuositatem, the document on the laity, the Council makes clear that a Christian's responsibility for the life of the church results from baptism into Christ. The theology of the apostolate that undergirded the Catholic Action movement spoke of the participation of the laity in the apostolate of the hierarchy. The Council corrects that theoretical understanding: all God's People are responsible for the Good News. The institutional church still has much to do to make its restructured story more faithful to the church's new root metaphor. That is not easy for an institution when "institution" itself is the metaphor that is being displaced as the root metaphor. Nor have the laity learned to wear "People of God" like an old shoe yet. The leather still squeaks a little, but the fit is becoming more and more comfortable.

In no institution's life is social reconstruction easy, but all must do it to live. For an institution that understands itself as semper reformanda (always under requirement to reshape itself), on-going social reconstruction is even more pressing. So often the "dangerous memories" are precisely those that demand conversion. They are not dangerous to a community's real life, only to its overly settled order.

This, then, is a very important part of the picture. Tell the baptized, "You, all of you, are People of God; and you, all of you, are responsible for the Good News." Tell them this often enough and they begin to believe in themselves as church. Then, when their needs and desires are not sufficiently ministered to under the older metaphoric dispensation, these People with their new image will see to it that Christian communities have the leadership and ministries they require. They will create a new dispensation. This is already happening in very large ways. The People of God are re-gathering themselves.

I want to offer, by way of an analogy, a reflection upon the distinction between lay and cleric, and upon other notions central to this book. After moving from one house to another several times in the course of a half dozen years, I recognized an interesting phenomenon in the new kitchen. With hundreds of items in boxes and bags, decisions had to be made about which items were to go in which drawers, in which cabinets, and on which shelves. Decisions like this are not merely random. They respond to practical need and to the "style" of the cooks who will use the kitchen. "Style," of course, is close to a person's identity. Yet they are arbitrary decisions, because there are thousands of possible arrangements. The day after everything has been put away it is already possible to begin saying, "it goes there." Given a few days more, it is possible to feel irritated when "something isn't where it belongs." The irritation is a response to disorientation, to interrupted expectation.

Sociologists call this phenomenon the social construction of reality; in the case of the kitchen it is the social construction of order. We very soon hide even from ourselves the constructed nature of what we ourselves have made, and we live as though the order exists independently: "It goes there," rather than "I have chosen for good reasons to locate it there." Two familiar ways of hiding the constructed nature of order are with philosophy and religion. If we can somehow demonstrate that the desirable social order is in harmony with cosmic order, we have ontological reasons why "it goes there." Or if we can account for order by relating its patterns to the narrative structure of a religious deep story, then we have a religiously ultimate reason why "it goes there." Peter Berger calls this religious

shelter for social construction a "sacred canopy." Every institution requires structures of ordering, norming and authorizing to
be faithful to its *raison d'etre*. Every institution is also wary of
allowing that order's constructed origin a vivid daily appearance.

Already in the historical life of Jesus, normative ways of being
among his disciples are being generated. Still more order is generated after the Easter event when the disciples are making it
on their own without the physical presence of Jesus. They are
still a group within Judaism, but with identity and order. Decisions are made about order in the communities of Jesus, and the
order gets names: *episcopus* ("overseer" who becomes bishop);
presbyteros ("elder" or "trusted community member" or "local
leader" who later becomes priest); *diakonos* ("servant" who later
becomes deacon), etc. This order does not come from Jesus but
from a community's historically and culturally conditioned social response to his Good News. This "social reconstruction" interpretation of aspects of early church order does not demean its
normative importance in Christian life. What is stressed is the
symbiotic relationship between faith and culture, and the
worldly condition of God's initiatives among us. God takes us
where we are. God's Spirit works in and through us in all our
respective worlds, and that includes our socially constructed
worlds. It is no less God's work because it is also ours, and it is
no less ours because it is also God's.

After the First Jewish War and the destruction of the temple
in 70 C.E., Christian communities forge an institutional identity separate from Judaism. In the latter decades of the first century, further decisions are made about "where it goes." House
churches become a normative way in which early communities
structure their life together. That the leader of the community
thereby also presides at eucharist seems to be part of the early
order. As the structuring of power becomes more complex, the
eucharistic presider begins to lose a sense of natural connectedness to the daily social functioning of the community. The distinction between lay and cleric does not seem to come from Jesus

but from 4th and 5th century decisions that have since been ontologized and sacred canopied.

The movements described in this book address many of the issues named in this kitchen-foray into the social construction of reality: house church forms of community and their patterns of leadership, ministry, and connectedness to other communities; eucharist and its celebration; the power/order distinction between lay and cleric. Remembering the socially constructed character of many aspects of settled ecclesial order is sometimes a dangerous memory for that settled order. As we explore in this book some new imagination about forms of discipleship, it is helpful to remember the socially constructed nature of some of the earlier models with which it contrasts. Though perhaps embarrassing, it is healthy for us writing the book to remind ourselves that in spite of ourselves we too shall be in search of sacred canopies (e.g., our memory of the house church) and cosmic legitimation (e.g., typologies from the social sciences).

A Shift in Imagination

In the previous section, we spoke of a shift in root metaphor. This section addresses a fundamental shift in how religious people imagine the world, a shift in images about what is religious, what is non-religious, and how those are related. As we shall see, how this world is imagined has influenced Christian understandings of "lay" and "clerical," and has therefore impacted significantly upon the narrative structure of Christian life in the Catholic church. The intentional Christian community movement is an alternative narrative for church that not only signals a change in the church's root metaphor, but in many ways signals the shift in imagination that we will trace in this chapter.

The paradigm for understanding "religious" and "non-religious" that has dominated Western Christian thought is inherited from the Greek world where the Christian mind on this matter was incubated. In the Greek world view, God's being is imagined to be radically different from historical temporal being. God is changelessly perfect, while the rest of reality is changefully imperfect. Rather than accepting our changefulness and temporality as the irreducible character of our finitude, we have sought to transcend them by coming to rest in the changelessness of God, as Augustine's oft quoted aspiration reflects: "Our hearts are ever restless until they rest in Thee." In popular religious language, we have often spoken about "this world" and "the other world," and about God as "totally other." The scriptural foundations for these images are to be found more in John's Gospel, where the Greek imagination has a larger impact, than in the synoptic Gospels.

In the framework of imagining the world in this way, the officially designated religious leaders (the hierarchy) are to be primarily concerned with the higher spiritual realm, and the laity with the temporal realm. It is not that laity are not to be spiritual, but it is they whose time and energies are explicitly directed to "secular" concerns, which are not the primary responsibility of priests and bishops. Thus, there are two kinds of reality: religious and secular; and clerical and lay reality are understood in ways that reflect this two-world paradigm.

In modern thought, there has been a shift towards a one-world view. There are two ways to get a one-world view. The first is to deny everything that used to be denominated as supernatural; then only one kind of reality is left. The second approach to a one-world view is to think of God and history as naturally related, naturally interconnected, mutually involved, and of temporal reality and human history as theatre for the drama of redemption.[5] God is presumed to be able to change, and thus God's experience assumes a temporal character. What it means for God to be God doesn't change. However, that is a very abstract side of God. But how God is God with us is forever changing its shape, as God seriously and intimately relates to every detail of the world and of human history. That's the concrete God, the pre-eminently relational God. Frankly, this understanding is quite of a piece with the biblical understanding of God. No Jew in the time of Jesus is likely to have wondered whether there is a pathos in God that feels our feelings, or whether God adjusts to our experience in his initiatives in our lives.

The philosophy of Martin Heidegger has had a very significant impact upon how contemporary theologians understand the theological task and interpret the Christ-event. Although Heidegger was raised a Catholic and spent a short time in the Jesuit novitiate, his philosophical work never directly addresses God questions. His major work is a sustained analysis of the essential connection between being and time. Near the very end of this work, tucked away in a footnote, Heidegger suggests that his analysis of the temporality of being may imply that God's eternity can be construed as "a more primordial temporality which is 'infinite'."[6] Heidegger's concern is to find a temporal way of affirming what non-temporal infinity used to affirm — in other words, not to create an alternative world to being-and-time. The American theologian, Schubert Ogden, has attempted to say what such temporal infinity might be like.[7] The point is not so much to enter the intricacies of philosophical theology, but to indicate that even in these areas there is serious question about a two-world way of imagining the relationship between the religious and the non-religious.

At a non-theoretical level, the very conduct of Christians today testifies to a new understanding. The French philosopher Merleau-Ponty has argued that human conduct is itself the primordial way of "thinking." And there is some interesting human behavioral thinking in the church these days. Clerics and members of religious congregations have become deeply engaged in politics in a number of places, most notably in South America, but in this country too (e.g., Robert Drinan, Mary Agnes Mansour). On the other hand, when clerics are unavailable for servicing the needs of small communities that spring up, the laity preach to themselves and sometimes lead themselves in eucharistic praise without bothering to ask whether their eucharist is a Eucharist with a capital "E." This phenomenon occurs sometimes in the Woman Church in the United States. These behaviors of both clerics and lay people are irregular sorties into the specific territory of the other, according to mainstream Catholic institutional understanding.

Two conclusions are possible. The first is that there is massive misunderstanding, and that the respective roles of laity, and of clerics and religious must be reaffirmed because these people are confused. The second is that these behaviors reflect a way of thinking about the world that does not acknowledge the two-world view of temporal and non-temporal, of secular and religious. William Burrows notes that several Christians in Papaua, New Guinea, speaking out of their cultural perception, thought

it was inconceivable that religion and politics should not march hand in hand. The western notion of their separation was demonic, for it split apart the form and substance of culture. Their position was one of terror at the thought of a religious world where religion and politics would be related as the sacred to the profane.[8]

This way of thinking appears to be emerging in the conduct of small intentional Christian communities throughout the world.

We took the expression "Dangerous Memories," from the work of Johannes Metz. One of the most dangerous of those memories is that there is a double composition to following Christ: the mystical and the political. There is not first the mystical and then the political; rather, how we should be in the world together, in all our social structures, is part of the reality of who God is for us, and is of an immediate piece with our experience of God. The political is of the substance of the mystical. We shall return to this theme in a sustained way in chapter six.

Within the Council itself there was movement on the two-world issue. In *Lumen Gentium*, early in the Council, the dualism is stressed:

A secular quality is proper and special to lay people . .
. [they] seek the Kingdom of God by engaging in temporal affairs and by ordering them according to God's
plan. . . [while] those in holy orders . . . are
chiefly and professionally ordained to the sacred ministry. (para. 31)

The pastoral constitution on the Church, *Gaudium et Spes*, has
very little dualism left:

What does the Church think about human life? What recommendations seem needful for the upbuilding of contemporary society? What is the ultimate significance of
human activity throughout the world? People are waiting
for an answer to these questions. From the answers it will
be increasingly clear that the people of God and the
human race in whose midst it lives render service to each
other. Thus the mission of the Church will show its religious, and by that very fact, its supremely human character. (para. 11)

The tension between "religious" and "supremely human" has
been removed. Politics, for example is surely one of the "supremely human" ways in which basic human needs are addressed
(or neglected). It is worth recalling that Thomas Aquinas
treated politics as a virtue under the major heading of pru-
dence.[9] Johannes Metz's presentation of the dangerous liberating memory of Jesus also clearly demonstrates the political
character of all Christian theology.[10]

Similarly, in *Gaudium et Spes* the Church agrees with the
judgment that "all things on earth should be related to human
life as their center and crown" (para. 12). We are made in God's
image, but it is we-of-the-earth that are in God's image, and we
cannot turn our face from history without turning our face from
God. By the end of the Council, then, the Church had committed
itself to history perhaps as never before.

A defining mark of the intentional Christian community movement is precisely that small groups of followers of Jesus have committed themselves quite radically to the redemption of human history. Whether one says the word "political" or not, the transformation of historical experience cannot but deeply involve the agents of transformation in political and economic realities.

We are far from having discovered from our recent experience (it isn't historically thick enough yet) how "lay" and "clerical" are to be re-interpreted, or even if the categories are helpful. Perhaps we need to recall that "cleric" names the leadership function (or at least it should) more fundamentally than it names a particular structure in the church's body politic. There is, to be sure, a character to Christian community leadership; however, the character of leadership can only be understood in tandem with the character of the community led. Clearly, our understandings of community and leadership are undergoing evolution and development today under the pressure of a new imagination about how "religious" and "non-religious" are to be related. It simply cannot be that leadership is religious and atemporal while the community led is secular and temporal!

Meanwhile, small communities of committed Christians are plowing into the immediacies of history with uncommon compassion, and often with a vigor which unnerves political structures that stand in violation of human dignity.

The Creative Transformation of Human History

It is certainly not the case that only now has the modern Church addressed the redemption of historical experience. Pope Leo XIII moved the mind of the Church solidly towards deep concern for social justice. What does seem different, however, is that the context within which the commitment is interpreted is increasingly a one-world view and not a two-world view. That makes the earlier distinction between lay and clerical responsibility to history wobbly. It sometimes feels that clerics, by their engagement in political realities, have begun to sacramentalize to laity the Church's newly pitched love for history, while lay leadership and lay ministries have begun to sacramentalize to hierarchy new modes of being for institutional Christian leadership.

In Latin America, the episcopal conferences at Medellin and Puebla charted that church upon a path from which there is no likely return. Some polarization has resulted, not only within the Latin American church, but within the large Catholic church itself. The basic Christian community movement there is composed mostly of the lower classes, especially the very poor, the disenfranchised, the marginated, the severely under-privileged. The politicization of Christian community is a direct result of a change of metaphor and a change of imagination: we are God's People and as such we cannot imagine a religious world in which unjust social structures are not a primary object of evangelization. The Latin American bishops expressed this in terms of a "preferential option for the poor."

The Vatican's uneasiness about liberation theology in Latin America is common knowledge. A first instruction on liberation theology from Cardinal Ratzinger was very negative towards the movement and its alleged Marxist underpinnings. Juan Luis Segundo published a detailed and theologically meticulous response to the Ratzinger document: *Theology and the Church: A Response to Cardinal Ratzinger and a Warning to the Whole Church.*[11]

Through patient (and probably impatient) dialogue between the Brazilian hierarchy and the Vatican, deeper understand-ings have been forged, out of which a quite supportive second in-struction on liberation theology emerged. One issue has become clearer: the use of "class struggle" as a category of social analysis does not constitute an acceptance of a Marxist ideology. The supportive personal letter of Pope John Paul II to Brazilian church leadership witnesses to the importance of dialectic com-

munity within the church itself. There is no doubt that liberation theology also has a surer grasp of its Christian task as a result of this same dialectic conversation. A mark of all true conversation is that all participants in it are called to conversion.

Because the intentional Christian community movement is a
world wide movement, we are listening to some of the experience beyond American shores. However, in this book our focus is
primarily upon the intentional Christian community movement
in the United States. In this country as well a new agenda for
the Church has emerged with surprising speed. In the sixties
and early seventies a new social and communal awareness
burgeoned in this country. Religious commitment was a source
of immense energy for both the racial justice movement and the
peace movement. People active in these movements were learning to gather themselves together in new ways. The communes
of the counter-culture were an experiment. They were not very
successful as a viable model for enduring community, but they
were effective in raising an issue that remains: the communal
context for caring about how life goes. During this same period
of our American story, we began hearing about sensitivity sessions, T-groups, communication workshops, etc. Important
pockets of American culture were acquiring skills necessary for
listening to the experience of those who suffer. In the last dozen
years, the drama of the counter-culture has dissipated, but
many of its better instincts have been quietly assimilated. (One
of the authors of this volume was a doctoral student in Berkeley
in the sixties and seventies, watched "People's Park" get rebuilt,
tried to help guide the student anger unleashed by the Kent
State killings, and saw the agonies and the ecstasies of small
groups in Haight-Asbury).

We have suggested above that in the years since Vatican II,
laity and hierarchy have often learned from each other. Without
the assimilation of communal impulses from those remarkable,
terrible, beautiful post-conciliar years of our American history,
American bishops may not have had the impulse to gather and
regather in Collegeville, Minnesota, to listen to one another's

experience and seek genuine community among themselves.

Gaudium et Spes says that "The People of God believes that it is led by the Spirit of the Lord, who fills the earth . . . It labors to decipher the authentic signs of God's purpose in the happenings, needs, and desires in which this People has a part along with other people of our age" (para. 11). So we hear God's purpose as we listen to people's needs and desires. In that spirit, United States bishops have begun to formulate an agenda for our American Church, and their new practice of open, learning conversation is a landmark in hierarchical behavior — it is a behavioral change that signals a new understanding of how official leadership relates to the historical lives of those led. The teacher as learner conditions the learner who in turn is teacher. These "learned" (from listening) teachers are focusing the care of American Catholics on the issues of peace and war, nuclear disarmament, and the role of women in culture and in the church. And, as Andrew Greeley's studies have demonstrated, the resultant pastoral letter (with all its hearings, open discussion, revisions, and attendant publicity) has wrought a remarkable transformation of Catholic conscience.[12] The second pastoral addresses economic policies and social justice. On this the bishops have been willing to risk some strong, prophetic positions which place the American story itself under critical review.

A notable shift is occurring in the leadership of the American hierarchy, and in that of other countries as well. The shift accompanies the development of national and regional espicospal conferences. Communities are always situated within larger contexts than themselves, with which they cannot but interact. The leader of a community, therefore, has two spokesperson roles. He/she must sometimes help the community understand the larger context, i.e., interpret the larger to the smaller. At other times she/he must help the larger group understand the experience of the small group, i.e., interpret the smaller to the larger. During our memory, we have usually experienced the bishops as interpreting Rome to the local churches. Increasingly, and this is the shift, the bishops are equally inter-preting the experience of the local churches to Rome (as have the Brazilian bishops). Both interpreter roles are necessary.

At this writing, American bishops have begun open hearings across the continent to listen to women's voices, for one can only interpret accurately that to which he/she has listened deeply. It is their intention to focus pastoral attention upon the evolving, developing role of women in culture and in the church. This is surely one of the most sensitive issues in the Catholic church because, finally, criteria for membership in the institutional power structure are being subjected to critical scrutiny in the light of the Good News of Jesus Christ.

These three issues — nuclear disarmament, economic policy, and the feminist movement — are precisely the issues which most often galvanize the small intentional Christian com-munities that are forming in the United States. In chapter six, we will focus more closely upon the social, political, and economic characteristics of all human life which the Gospel puts under requirement.

The three issues named by the United States bishops, after having learned them in part from listening to some of the American People of God, are immensely complex. Not only that, these issues are some of the most deeply embedded structures of our cultural systems. In short, the People of God are facing off with megastructures. The individual person cannot but feel utterly helpless in such a face-off; yet when People rather than person face off, there is hope.

Once the People of God take seriously that they are a missioned people, and once they focus upon such issues as the United States bishops have identified, what next?   How are they not to despair of transformation, before the impersonality and unwieldiness of the megastructures?   In their book on mediating structures, *To Empower People*, Peter Berger and John Neuhaus note that "many who handle it more successfully than most have access to institutions that mediate between the two spheres [the private individual and the public megasystem]".[13] They describe mediating structures as "those institutions standing between the individual in his private life and the large institutions of public life."[14] Intentional Christian communities have the potential for being such mediating structures. If Christians are politicized by the very character of Christian existence, if they must therefore make a difference in how history goes, and if they are, finally, to maintain hope for historical transformation, the mediating group seems entirely necessary. Later we will use these two sociological categories, intentional community and mediating group, further to characterize the kind of community this book addresses. Now, however, let us remember the experience of the very early church. It is a dangerous memory, and like most "dangerous" memories, it is also a memory full of solace, full of grace and power. It is the retrieval of our Great Story.

The House Church in Early Christianity

The Letters of Paul and the Acts of the Apostles both make clear that the early communities of Christians ordinarily gathered in the homes of members, especially larger homes. However, they were not doing strange, surreptitious things. Gatherings of this sort had clear precedents in both Jewish and Greek life. To understand the house church phenomenon, it will help to look briefly at these models.

To begin with, part of Jewish ritual in the time of Jesus as well as now is the Seder meal, celebrated in the home with other families—a larger group than the single family and a smaller group than an entire synagogue. Jesus celebrated the last supper in the upper room of someone's house. In fact, the house was a regular place for community gathering and ritual. Early Jewish Christians would have found house gatherings for community quite a "natural" idea.

Further, there is much archaeological evidence that large rooms in private houses sometimes functioned as the regular meeting place for the entire Jewish synagogue (the word synagogue, like the word church, originally named the gathering of people and not the place of gathering). Today if you go about twenty minutes away from Jerusalem to the small village of Ein Kerem, you will see a home in the center of the small square whose large room at the lower level is the synagogue from which song and prayer pour out every Shabbas.

We also know now that in the time of Jesus, the Pharisees formed table fellowship groups, called *Haveroth*. Later Christian polemics with Pharisees which find their way backwards into the Gospels obscure how close the teachings of Jesus actually are to those of the Pharisees. The Gospels, in what are probably historically accurate recollections, place Jesus at meals with the Pharisees, which could not happen without significant, though perhaps not total, congruence between their teachings.

As a wandering teacher, therefore, Jesus' wont is not an isolated pattern.[15] A wandering teacher and his principal disciples move from town to town. Though largely unnoticed (by men!) the Gospels indicate that women are included in Jesus' traveling group. In local areas where they stop, friends put them up. Gerd Theissen speaks of two social forms of following Jesus, the disciples who travel with him, and the local sympathizers, who are likely to have been the earliest household units of Christian discipleship.[16] Although identification cannot be made with absolute certainty, it seems very likely that archaeological finds in Capernaum, the adult home of Jesus, disclose a first century Christian house church (the so-called "House of Peter") over which a fourth century Byzantine church was built.[17] Clearly, then, the development of house church units has roots in Jewish life itself.

The Greek world too had developed some patterns that made the house church a quite natural phenomenon.[18] In 5th century BCE Athens, the Greek citizen has a direct voice in the affairs of a democratic polity—this context is called *politeia*. The other major context is home life, or *oikonomia*. By the first century of the Christian era, government has become so complex that citizens feel shut out from public life.[19] Since many people do not want home to become the only social context for daily life, a new kind of gathering develops, *koinonia*. *Koinonia* is a gathering of people from a variety of backgrounds with some common interests. It is a voluntary association, or a partnership of sorts. The guild is one form of *koinonia*, people with common professional interests. Their gatherings sometimes include shared meals, e.g., to celebrate the birthday of a member. There are both formal, professional relations, and also voluntary loyalty and concern. These groups normally vary in size from a dozen to 30 or 40, rarely more than a hundred.

Even apart from guild-like associations, the Greek "household" is larger than a nuclear family. Besides parents and children, the household includes slaves and former slaves, hired workers, professional business acquaintances, tenants, and other close associates. "To be a part of a household was thus to be part of a larger network of relations . . ."[20] People who gather for whatever reason can easily get a charter for their association. Precisely because groups have a power that individuals lack, government is not always delighted at the franchised smaller groups. Even if their character is not explicitly political, they are a political presence, as Abraham Malherbe notes:

> In New Testament times the household was regarded as a basic political unity . . . The closeness of the household unit offered the security and sense of belonging not provided by larger political and social structure. The head of the household has a degree of legal responsibility for his charges, but the solidarity of the group was based more on economic, and especially psychological, social, and religious factors.[21]

When the expression "house church" is used throughout this book, it never refers only to a Christian nuclear family, but always to a larger relational web of people. As we shall see later, in our contemporary American experience we often feel deep alienation from political processes and helplessness in our desire to transform unjust structures — thus the "mediating group" becomes vital. But we are not accustomed to *koinonia* gatherings in the ancient Greek sense. In fact, we tend to protect our privacy and autonomy. The house church movement in the United States represents our attempt once again to take some destiny into our hands, to assume responsibility for the power of the relational web, to rediscover how much more each of us is together than apart. As Christians, we are indeed One Body, and need living em-Body-ments of that reality.

It is not surprising, then, that the household became the model for the gathering of Christians. Often, it is a whole household that is baptized, that of Stephanas (I Cor 10:2) or Cornelius (Acts 10:2). The house is a gathering place. When Paul addresses the issue of the Lord's supper, he speaks of coming together in a particular house as coming into church, that is, into the gathering of Christians (I Cor 11:18-20). From Acts we also know of the households of Lydia (16:15), the Philippian jailer (16:31-34) and Crispus (18:8). Paul also refers to households in his Letter to the Romans, those of Aristobulus (16:10) and Narcissus (16:11).

Paul mentions not only individual household churches, but also churches in the plural, such as "the churches in Galatia" (Gal 1:2), "the churches in Asia" (I Cor 16:19) or the "churches in Macedonia" (II Cor 8:1). It is also clear that in those places where there were multiple house churches, they sometimes met together as a single church, as in Corinth (I Cor 14:23). The sort of letter Paul wrote to the Romans, with messages to many people, makes it seem likely that it was to be read at a gathering of all the churches in the area. So the *koinonia* was not only among members of one house church, but among the multiple house churches in a city. Further, the collections which Paul took up were then redistributed, indicating the further linkage of churches with one another from city to city and country to country. In respect to maintaining connection, Malherbe refers to the great amount of traveling that was done in the first century. In his letter to the Romans, Paul names 26 people he knows from previous contacts, though he himself has not yet been to Rome. Malherbe says that :

> Traveling Christians . . . must have contributed to the formation of a network by which information about churches was communicated. In this way they would have contributed to the unity of the church and to whatever continuities characterized early Christians.[22]

The house church appears to have been the basic unit of ecclesial life in the early centuries, indeed into the fourth century when Christianity became the state religion and could function publicly.

In the early centuries, house churches would also have been the natural places of formation for those who were to provide major leadership for the church once the original apostles had died. Not surprisingly, the host of the household church was often the most influential member of a house church. [23]

In this context, a further speculation seems invited. We simply do not have any witness from the New Testament as to who presides at the eucharist of the early Christians. What seems highly probable, however, is that whoever leads the community also presides at its eucharist.[24] Now some of the household leaders in the early church are women. That does indeed make us wonder whether women might have presided at eucharist! Given the fact that there is precedent for a woman as leader of a Jewish synagogue,[25] and that the synagogue model shaped early Christian structures, we have additional reason to wonder. But this is a question to which no historical records offer an explicit reply.

The house church, it must be insisted, was not a piece or part of church. It *was* church, even as the network of churches was also church. Paul does not say to the church at Corinth that "you are *part* of the Body of Christ," rather, "you *are* the Body of Christ" (I Cor 12:27). Reflecting on this, Banks says "this suggests that wherever Christians are in relationship, there is the body of Christ in its entirety, for Christ is truly and wholly present there through his spirit (v. 13). This is a momentous truth."[26] In the final part of this chapter, we want to elaborate still more upon what makes a house church, or any form of intentional Christian community, be truly a church.

Truly Church

The Youth Club, the Altar Society, the individual nuclear family are social groups and they are Christian, but they are not fully unto themselves churches. There are four characteristics of any Christian group without which a gathering cannot be itself truly church (though it can be truly part of a church). These are: 1) *koinonia*/community; 2) *diakonia*/service or mission; 3) *kerygma*/Gospel-rooted; and 4) *leitourgia*/eucharist. Because the small Christian communities that are springing up across the globe, including those in the United States, aspire to be church in the fullest sense, we will look at these characteristics.

Koinonia

Every church is *koinonia* in two important senses. It is community in that the members of a church are concerned about each other's welfare. They are linked one to another by their care. In this respect, they are similar to what sociologists call a primary group: they are marked by voluntary bonding.

Secondly, every unit must sense its belongingness to other units, all of whom confess the same Jesus Christ. This is community in the extended sense. In the early churches, each community chose its own leaders and ministers. When one church laid hands upon leaders to incorporate them officially into the leadership structure of the church, leaders from other communities participated in the ritual in order to witness to the continuity of faith between the ordaining church and the other churches. Without this kind of interconnectedness, a house church would quickly become idiosyncratic. This is always a danger: Paul has to remind the different house churches in Corinth that they should never get their identity from the leader of the house church, for that divides Christ up (I Cor 1:10:17). Their identity, and therefore their unity, is rather in their baptism.

Diakonia

Fundamental to the message of Jesus are the consequences he sees of the Fatherhood of God. It makes all of us God's children. The deepest truth about us, therefore, is that all of us are brothers and sisters. *Diakonia* names the ministries of service whereby the needs of the brothers and sisters are ministered to by others of the sisters and brothers. Here we are not talking primarily about the needs which come from a desire for qualitatively strong interpersonal relationships (which koinonia embraces), but of genuine material needs, of needs relating to social structures, etc.

We cannot ignore need among our brothers and sisters any place in the world. No community, therefore, may limit its *diakonia* to its immediate group, but must always attend to the larger social and political realities in which it finds itself. These are the direct consequences of God's parenthood of us all. Jesus knew from his religious experience of God what the human life should look like. Johannes Metz speaks of Jesus standing up for the glory of God in the midst of the individual and social contradictions of life.[27] Because of this there is a mystical and sociopolitical composition to following Christ. *Diakonia* names the material, social, and political service a community renders to the needs of its immediate members and to brothers and sisters who live beyond its immediate confines. We must serve wherever there is need for service. Every true church experiences this sense of mission or service to both its immediate membership and to the larger world.

Kerygma

The story of Jesus is not only biographical of one person, but is paradigmatic for all the followers of Jesus. It is a story that gets remade many times in many new circumstances. It is the Great Story, or the Deep Story, for the People of God. It makes history by being re-interpreted and re-incarnated century by century, year by year, day by day. That accumulating story then becomes as much part of the Great Story as the original story. All the churches have in common that they interpret their present story in conversation with the Great Story, and make new history. *Kerygma* is the name for the Great Story whose proclamation gathers together a people of faith. For it is the proclaimed Great Story that every true church shares with every other true church.

The two disciples on the way to Emmaus encountered Jesus the evening of the resurrection. They recognized him in the breaking of the bread (Lk 24:35). Before Christians had a separate identity apart from Judaism, they both prayed in the temple and went to their house churches to break bread together (Acts 2:46). *Leitourgia*/liturgy names public ritual acts. For Catholic Christians, the central ritual act has always been the breaking of the bread in Eucharist. Each gathering unit of Christians that is church is a eucharist-celebrating unit. This does not mean a family or a small group that has an occasional mass at home, but rather a group that is normally and regularly a eucharist-celebrating group by its character.

This mark of the genuine ecclesial unit presents a problem and a challenge in today's church. In the early communities, leaders come from the communities they served, and because they are leaders they preside at eucharist. In this theology, ordination is to community leadership, and leadership of eucharist is derivative from leadership of community. In a later theology, which has predominated during most of the church's history, that relationship is reversed. Ordination means empowerment for eucharist, and derivative from that the ordained person than becomes a community's leader.[28]

there are not enough priests for the thousands of small communities. Most of the time these communities have liturgy of the word together, and in the rarer moments when a priest can be there they have eucharist. Thus, even though they do not have eucharist as often as they would like, their orientation is clearly eucharistic. They have the ecclesial characteristic of *leitourgia*.

Still other groups have their natural leader preside at the Lord's Supper without trying to make a case out of it. Leonardo Boff says that if a community without an ordained priest should designate its leader to preside at the Lord's Supper, "this community would celebrate, truly, really, and sacramentally, The Lord's Supper."[29] In his opinion (which is surely not the universal opinion in the church), this arrangement would be outside the church's discipline (*praeter ordinem*), but not against the intention of the discipline (*contra ordinem*) nor against the church (*contra ecclesiam*). For him this is true, because every church has an apostolic right to eucharist that supercedes any church-made regulations that would deprive a church of eucharist. What is being named here is the plight of many house churches regarding their *leitourgia*. They are clearly eucharistic bodies in their intentionality, and must struggle often to be that in fact.

We are not hearkening to the experience of the early church as alone normative for today's experience. There are valid models in every century, and all of them have authority. The second century model has no intrinsic superiority over the twelfth century or the twentieth century just because it is earlier. However, a new experiment in ecclesiality is afoot in our world today, and it is helpful to interpret the movement in conversation with another time. Since we are a communion of saints, our *koinonia* today is fellowship also with the house churches in Capernaum, Corinth, Ephesus and Rome.

Perhaps the point is this: house church is a very helpful metaphor for today's contemporary experiment with small Christian communities. A metaphor says one thing is like another — and many things about house gatherings all around the world are like the house gatherings of the earliest communities. What they all have, those who are truly units of church, are: *koinonia, diakonia, kerygma,* and *leitourgia.* But in every metaphor there is always a secret "it also is not like . . ." Our situation is not identical with that of the early church. We are doing a new thing by responding to our Great Story as best we can today in the context of our American story. In the next chapter, we shall have a bird's eye view of this new experiment with our Great Story, across the globe and in our own land.

Additional Resources

Church

The Church (Lumen Gentium) and *The Church Today (Gaudium et Spes)* from Vatican II. Note the move from a clear two-world view in the first to a struggling affirmation of one-world in the second document. Also worth noting is the strong contrast between the ecclesiology of Vatican I and Vatican II. Although there is only a first draft of a dogmatic constitution on the church from Vatican I (the Council closed prematurely before this and other items were formally decided), it does fairly represent the Council members. Notice the chasmic distinction made between the church and society in chapter 3: "[While] the Church has all the qualities of a true society . . . the Church is not a member or a part of any other society whatsoever . . . But it is so perfect in itself that although it is distinct from all other human societies, it is nevertheless far superior to them." Here the two world view with all its ecclesial ramifications is clearly in evidence. *Gaudium et Spes* is a remarkable contrast, a sign of a different time.

Avery Dulles, *Models of the Church* (Garden City: Doubleday, 1974). This book remains a jewel for its treatment of the decisive role of models for how we understand church and relate to it. In connection with the subject matter of this present book, cf. esp. chapters 1 (the role of models), 2 (institution) and 3 (church as community). Thomas S. Kuhn's book, *The Structure of Scientific Revolutions* (Chicago: Univ. of Chicago Press, 1976), discusses how our ways of seeing the world (paradigms) determine what questions we are able to ask, what data we are able to notice, etc. A paradigm shift makes way for new questions, new data, and finally new ways of seeing the world and being in the world. As the sociology of knowledge demonstrates, ways of seeing world *construct* ways of being in the world. A brief, clear treatment of this can be found in Peter L. Berger's *The Sacred Canopy* (Garden City: Doubleday, 1969), chapter 1, "Religion and World Construction." We *make* the meanings out of which we live as we interpret experience. Paradigms are central to our interpretive acts. It is our contention in this book that the intentional Christian community movement is a response to a serious shift in metaphor and imagination, and can be seen as a new social construction of ecclesial reality.

Metaphor

Sallie McFague, *Metaphorical Theology* (Philadelphia: Fortress 1982). While this book is on God language rather than church language, the first two chapters are excellent discussions of the role of metaphor in human understanding, and how a change in metaphor changes experience. Paul Ricoeur's *The Rule of Metaphor* (Toronto: Univ. of Toronto Press, 1981) is perhaps the contemporary classic on the matter. Metaphors are not like fables: when you know what a fable means, you don't need it anymore, but a metaphor is not substitutable. Nor are metaphors mere embellishments. Metaphors give information which cannot be given another way, and have affective and performative as well as cognitive content. Every metaphor says one thing "is like another thing." But since there is not mere identity between the two items, there is always a secret "it is also not like the other thing." In philosophy or theology we are in serious trouble when we forget a metaphor's "it is not like . . ." Theology's prime way of forgetting the "is not like" is by ontologizing a metaphor. Therefore, even as we celebrate the emergence of "People of God" as a new root metaphor, we must not violate it by forgetting that it is only a partial broaching of the deeper reality of ecclesial existence.

House Churches

While it is clear that houses churches were the normal mode of church life in the early centuries, there is not a lot of exact information about how they actually functioned. The studies listed below represent the best scholarship available from the past half-dozen years. These studies are helpful for understanding how house church can be a useful metaphor for contemporary intentional Christian communities. However, in the early centuries one did not have an option between the house church and some other forms of ecclesial life, such as an urban parish of 1,800 families with a large church building, a pastor and one or two assistants. Contemporary house churches are an alternative to established structures, and in that respect "are not like" the house churches of the early years.

Robert Banks, *Paul's Idea of Community: The Early House Churches in their Historical Setting* (Grand Rapids: Eerdmans, 1980). This is probably the best single reference for the house church.

Abraham J. Malherbe, *Social Aspects of Early Christianity* (Philadelphia: Fortress, 1983), esp. chapter 3, "House Churches and Their Problems."

Wayne A. Meeks, *The First Urban Christians: The Social World of the Apostle Paul* (New Haven: Yale, 1983), esp. chapter 1, "The Urban Environment of Pauline Christianity," and chapter 3, "The Formation of the *Ekklesia*."

David N. Power, "Households of Faith in the Coming Church," *Worship*, 57/3 1983, pp. 237-254.

Notes

1. David Tracy has suggested understanding the Christian scriptures as literary classics. The classic stories "live" because there is in them such excess of meaning that they have yield century after century. Classic experiences may be understood analogously. They are ways of being in the world that are so rich that they can be explored over and over and continue in such conversation to generate meaning. The early church is a kind of classic text with which contemporary movements in the church converse, such as the small Christian community movement. The small community movement in the contemporary church does not mimic the house churches of the early centuries but rather evokes an array of new meanings in new historical circumstances. Cf. David Tracy, *The Analogical Imagination* (N.Y.: Crossroad, 1981), chapter 3, "The Classic."

2. Ivo Lorscheiter, cited in *Pro Mundi Vita*, 81/1980, p. 16.

3. Milan Kundera, *The Unbearable Lightness of Being* (N.Y. Harper & Row, 1984), pp. 11, 221.

4. The "living out" of a metaphor's implication is akin to what Paul Ricouer means when he speaks of a text's meaning as being "out in front" of the text. What we understand always impacts upon the world of possibility before us, and that projection is included in the meaning of what we know. A metaphor's meaning, therefore, is tightly bound up with the "living out" that it evokes. There is a world that a metaphor empowers to appear out in front of us — that is why a shift in metaphor for church is so loaded for the actual experience of being church. Cf. Robert M. Grant and David Tracy, *A Short History of the Interpretation of the Bible* (Philadelphia: Fortress, 1984), esp. chapter 16 (by Tracy), "Interpretation of the Bible and Interpretation Theory."

5. *The Church Today/Gaudium et Spes* is one of the most world-centered, creation-affirming documents of the Catholic church. For example, "The Council focuses its attention on the world of human beings, the whole human family along with the sum of those realities in the midst of which that family lives. It gazes upon the world which is the theatre of human history, and carries the marks of human energies, human tragedies and human triumphs . . ." (para. 2) Cf. also paragraphs 3, 12, and many other passages throughout the document.

6. Martin Heidegger, *Being and Time* (N.Y.: Harper & Row, 1962), p. 499, n. xiii.

7. Schubert M. Ogden, *The Reality of God* (N.Y.: Harper & Row, 1977), chapter V, "The Temporality of God."

8. William R. Burrows, *New Ministries: The Global Context* (Maryknoll: Orbis, 1981), p. 30.

9. *Summa Theologica* II-II, Q. 47, a. 11.

10. Johannes Metz, *Faith in History and Society: Towards a Practical Fundamental Theology* (N.Y.: Crossroad, 1980), esp. chapter 4, "The Concept of a Political Theology as a Practical Fundamental Theology." The entire book makes the point that Christian theology cannot be apolitical. Metz treated the topic earlier in a series of lectures on religious life, published as *Followers of Christ* (N.Y.: Paulist, 1978), esp. chapter 2, "The Time Is Now."

11. Juan Luis Segundo, *Theology and the Church: A Response to Cardinal Ratzinger and a Warning to the Whole Church* (Minneapolis: Winston, 1985). Segundo finds the Ratzinger instruction dangerous not just for liberation theology, but for contemporary theology generally, because it does not do justice to the socio-political nature of human existence.

12. Andrew Greeley, *American Catholics since the Council: An Unauthorized Report* (Chicago: Thomas More, 1985), pp. 93-94.

13. Peter J. Berger and John Neuhaus, *To Empower People: The Role of Mediating Structures in Public Policy* (Washington, D.C.: American Enterprise Institute for Public Policy Research, 1977), p. 3.

14. Berger/Neuhaus, 1977, p. 2.

15. Geza Vermes, *Jesus the Jew*, (Philadelphia: Fortress, 1981), pp. 58-62.

16. Gerd Theissen, *Sociology of Early Palestinian Christianity* (Philadelphia: Fortress, 1978), the two socials forms of response to Jesus are noted in chapter II,"The Role of Wandering Charismatics," and chapter III, "The Role of Sympathizers in the Local Communities."

17. Eric M. Meyers and James F. Strange, *Archaeology: The Rabbis and Early Christianity* (Nashville: Abingdon, 1981), pp. 128-130.

18. Robert Banks, *Paul's Idea of Community: The Early House Churches in Their Historical Setting* (Grand Rapids: Eerdmans, 1982), pp. 15-17.

19. Banks, 1982, p. 16.

20. Wayne Meeks, *The First Urban Christians: The Social World of the Apostle Paul* (New Haven: Yale, 1983), p. 30.

21. Abraham Malherbe, *Social Aspects of Early Christianity* (Philadelphia: Fortress, 1983), p. 69.

22. Malherbe, 1983, p. 65.

23. Marlherbe, 1983, p. 61.

24. Herve-Marie Legrand, "The Presidency of the Eucharist According to the Ancient Tradition," *Worship*, 53/5 (1979), pp. 413-438.

25. Bernadette Brooten, *Women Leaders in the Ancient Synagogue*, (Chico: Scholars Press, 1982).

26. Banks, 1982, p. 63.

27. Metz, 1978, p. 44.

28. Edward Schillebeeckx, *Ministry: Leadership in the Community of Jesus Christ* (N.Y.: Crossroad, 1981), and *The Church with a Human Face: A New Expanded Theology of Ministry* (N.Y.: Crossroad, 1985).

29. Leonardo Boff, *Ecclesiogenesis: The Base Communities Reinvent the Church* (Maryknoll: Orbis, 1986), p. 73. Boff's conclusions are of a piece with those of Schillebeeckx: the church may not impose a non-necessary restriction upon eucharistic presidency if that restriction deprives communities of eucharistic celebration. The right to eucharist is an apostolic right. Like any society, the church has the right to set guidelines and structures for community membership and leadership, so long as these do not contravene an apostolic right.

Chapter 2

HOUSE CHURCHES
IN MANY LANDS

The regathering of Christian people in the United States is the concern of this book. We want to know what is already happening, and how we can assist the emergence of a strong, indigenously American intentional Christian community movement. Of course, we Americans are not doing a unique thing in the Christian world today; when we regather we are doing what a lot of people across the globe are doing. It will be helpful for us to take a short look at these our companions in a shared experiment in ecclesial reality. "Companions" seems suddenly like such a right word, coming as it does form two Latin words, *cum/*with and *panis/*bread. Com-panions share bread. On the table of the earth, our many house churches are breaking bread together. As we do, we recognize Christ and we know one another. Our fellowship is large. It is growing. We are movement. We are a movement.

Though it is evident that the ICC movement is widespread, it would be a mistake to think of it as a homogeneous movement springing up everywhere. It is not homogeneous. And widespread doesn't mean "all over the place everywhere"; it means there are significant examples of it in enough places to suggest it is a movement.

33

There are vast differences between the house churches in Latin America and those in Africa, those in the third world and those in the first. Moreover, they have their own characteristics in Brazil, or Peru, or Mexico, etc., even though all are Latin American. They have their own expression in the 82 dioceses of eastern Africa, different from those of the Upper Volta. The expressions are different because there are different cultures, different histories, different issues, different politics, different economies, and different church traditions.

In *Community of Faith,* Evelyn and James Whitehead recommend a sociological understanding of "community" when used in the context of intentional Christian communities.[1] Because community is used so loosely to mean so many things, the description they suggest is very helpful for our purposes. There are two kinds of groups, which may be thought of as far ends of a spectrum. A primary group is one in which the bonding is very affective in character. It is a natural grouping, based upon family or friendship bonds. The quality of their interpersonal life is a primary concern. The other kind of group is a secondary group, with characteristics more like those of a formal organization. The secondary group exists for some purpose other than their own relationships. They may also do some interpersonal sharing, which would make their work more enjoyable. But they have a shared task, and that is their real reason for being a group. While a primary group like a family might also work together for some shared concern, like helping a neighbor, and while that would enrich their family life, it would still not be the reason why they are grouped as a family (or why friends are grouped as friends).

A "community" is a hybrid group because it has some characteristics of both the primary group and the secondary group. There is no innate superiority of primary, secondary, or hybrid groups; society needs all of them. A true Christian community, an ecclesial unit, is the hybrid form. Members of a Christian community have and express their care for each other as sisters and brothers in Christ. They know each other well enough to care personally and directly. In this, they are a primary group. Members of a Christian community also feel mission. They are in the world to help build the People of God. Their caring energy must flow beyond their immediate membership into the creative transformation of human history. In this, they are a secondary group. In the previous paragraph we noted how different are the house churches in the different cultures where they are growing up today. What they have in common is that sociologically they are the hybrid form called "community."

The amazing thing is that for whatever reasons and in whatever forms, **IT** is happening in our time in very many lands: small intentional groups with *koinonia, diakonia, kerygma,* and *leitourgia.* One begins to suspect that something stirs deep within the human spirit. Can the Spirit of God be anything but there in those poignant stirrings! In his very recent book, *Ecclesiogenesis,* Leonardo Boff speaks about the ICC movement as a re-invention of the church.[2] Christians who over the centuries have prayed for the gift of Spirit that enkindles fires in our hearts, and remakes the face of the earth, are not surprised that One who invented church on Pentecost can re-invent it whenever it is timely. History suggests that Pentecost is a moveable feast.

In our geographical tour of ICCs, we will look first at the Latin church and then the African church. Then we will visit the Philippine church which has some elements of both the Latin American and African experiences. We will then consider the situation in Europe, and turn finally to the church in the United States. The ICC movement has been reported upon over recent years in the *Pro Mundi Vita* bulletins from PMV's headquarters in Brussels, Belgium,[3] and those bulletins will often be our tour guide.

Latin America — Brazil

The real beginnings of a large movement are not easy to uncover. But Brazil is a good start. The widespread formation of intentional Christian communities has been underway there for about 20 years (with roots in even earlier initiatives). There are more ICCs in Brazil than in any other country of the world. Here, of course, the intentional Christian communities are usually called Basic Christian Communities (*communidades de base*), or Basic Ecclesial Communities.

The BCCs in Brazil probably have roots in organized efforts in the late 50's and early 60's to promote community evangelization in Barro do Pirai in Rio de Janeiro. Because there were not enough priests, lay catechists played a significant role. Radio schools were begun and radio liturgies were broadcast on Sundays. The Brazilian bishops designed a pastoral plan (for 1965-1970) that emphasized the importance of working with basic Christian community groups. However, the strongest support for this movement came from the Medellin conference of Latin American bishops in 1968, which faced the church in the direction of liberation theology and basic Christian communities. (We will return to both of these themes a little later.)

At this writing, there have been five major conferences of BCCs in Brazil.[4] They have grown in number and vigor. The themes of these assemblies themselves speak loudly about the nature of the enterprise. The first conference in Vitoria in 1975 focused on the theme, "A Church Born from the People through the Spirit of God." There were 80 participants. The second conference, in 1976, was also in Vitoria; its theme was, "The Church: A People on Its Way," and there were 100 participants. The third conference in Joao Pessoa in 1978 focused on "The Church: A People who Liberate Themselves," with 100 participants. The 1980 conference near Sao Paolo drew 300 persons from 18 states and 71 dioceses; its theme was "The Church: An Oppressed People Organizing Itself for Freedom." The 1984 conference was in Caninde on the theme, "Basic Ecclesial Communities: People United, the Seed of a New Society." There were 374 participants and all 14 regions of the Nation Episcopal Conference of Brazil were represented. Also participating were 15 theologians and economists and 33 bishops. There was an initial attempt to separate the theologians, priests and bishops from the lay people in the discussion, which the BCCs resisted. Bishop Fragoso asked when pastors would learn to be companions on the journey without silencing the voice of the people.

Put the conference themes together and you have quite a succinct description and theology of the BCC movement. These are people who are deeply conscious of being church. They have a sense of themselves as grassroots people who have responsibility for the destiny of the church in their world. God's Spirit is working through God's people, which is to be expected by a church that is always on its way. God became a people's God through the historical action of freeing the Hebrews from slavery and oppression, and that continues to be how God becomes our God. While redemption is God's initiative and cannot occur without God, it is also a co-operative venture between God and God's people, and it cannot happen without them. God's people organize their life of prayer, and also co-ordinate their resources and energies toward social transformation. They are united in their conviction that with God there can be a New Earth.

The number of participants at these five conferences is perhaps deceptive, because they are basically the key representatives of the larger movement. Current estimates suggest that there are between 80,000 and 150,000 of these small Christian communities in the Brazilian church. Not 150,000 persons, but 150,000 community units! What began, perhaps, as a deliberate church tool for evangelization in Brazil became a grassroots movement surging from marginated and disenfranchised lay Christians, and has emerged as a formidable influence upon the entire church. They are not merely tools for spreading church, but are themselves a new way of being church.

The BCC's are an active and transformative movement in much of Latin American now. Liberation theology is also widespread in its influence. However, we must consistently recall the complexity of the situation. The BCCs differ from country to country as they respond to and out of the particularities of their own cultural milieu. Equally, liberation theologians differ among themselves in how they approach the internal relation between Christian faith and the redemption of social, economic, and political systems. Guttierez, Segundo, Boff, Alves, etc., are certainly not of a single voice. The Vatican church and the Latin American church do not assign the same meanings to BCCs or to liberation themes in theology. There are not many historical paradigms for the church trying to evangelize "systems" in a large scale way — a recurring liberation theme. During most of Christian history, metanoia has been asked of individuals. Liberation theology and BCCs demand the conversion of systems as well: economic systems, social systems, political systems. The Latin American movements in this kind of theology and community receive rather broad support from the hierarchy. But we must also remember that the church is often a divided church on many of these issues.

The word "basic" in the Basic Christian Community is rich in multiple meanings. "Basic" names the origin of the movement: it comes right out of the energies, yearnings and commitments of basic people—it is a grassroots movement. "Basic" also names the movement's sense that it is grounded in the basics of the Christian Good News. It seeks to recover Jesus' reality as one anointed by God's Spirit to bring the Good News to the poor, to announce freedom for the enslaved, and to set the downtrodden free (Luke 4:18). These "basics" of the Good News are crucial for people who are desperately poor, systemically enslaved and downtrodden.

"Basic" also names the recovery of a foundational meaning of church. The church of Jesus Christ is intrinsically social. It calls people to live in community, to form community, to be formed by community. It calls for community to be a sacrament of Jesus Christ through its embodiment of the Good News. In a sense, the Christian person is indeed the basic "individual unit" of Christian sacrament: an individual Christian life configures Christian existence. And in another sense, Christian families and Christian friendships are the basic "social units" of Christian sacrament. But individuals, friends, and families are not community units; their individual and social existences must finally have community for their context. Neither individual persons, nor families and friends, have all four characteristics: *koinonia, diakonia, kerygma,* and *leitourgia.* In the profound sense of ecclesial reality as community, the basic Christian communities are the smallest community units of the church, its building blocks. Parish units are usually far too large to allow the kind of personal interaction necessary for them to be places of identity formation.

The ecclesiology that underpins the Rite of Christian Initiation for Adults is such a "basic" ecclesiology. The rite asks that a person who desires to become a Catholic be apprenticed to a small, active, i.e., "basic," Christian community. This phase, according to the rite, may last several years. Baptism is appropriate when the deep story of a catechumen's faith has been socialized in the Good News of Jesus Christ through the dynamics of mutuality in an intentional Christian community.

Basic Christian communities in Latin America, though diverse in character, are up to three things. First, they pray, worship, sing, explore the scriptures together; they attend to their spiritual lives. Second, they offer mutual support to one another, spiritually, materially, and emotionally. And thirdly, they pool their resources and unite their commitments for the social transformation of unjust structures.

We now turn our attention to Africa.

Africa

The social, economic and political structures of African life are, for the most part, significantly different from those in Latin America. The history of the church there is quite different. And so is the intentional Christian community movement. In Africa these units are more often called "small Christian Communities," "SCCs."

The SCC movement is strongest in Eastern Africa. In 1976, at a plenary conference of the bishops of Eastern Africa, building small communities was given a strong pastoral priority for the 82 dioceses of Kenya, Uganda, Tanzania, Zambia, and Malawi. One of the characteristics of the movement in Africa, distinguishing it from that of South America, is that the hierarchy itself has usually been the instigator of the movement (though there are exceptions to this, such as some grassroots efforts in the church in Zaire [5]).

Liberation from unjust social structures is not usually the key theme. The movement is rather deeply pastoral in nature, attending to community needs, and helping to develop an indigenously African ecclesial life. If there is tension between the Latin American church and Rome over political commitments, the edge between Rome and Africa tends to be over issues of the inculturation of church life in African modes and mores.

In the last decade over 10,000 SCCs have developed in the dioceses of Eastern Africa. That is certainly a notable achievement, and these communities have indeed contributed significantly to the deepening and "localizing" (indigenization) of African faith. But a problem that has plagued these particular African efforts is that one can't really create grassroots communities "from above." Grassroots communities get their inspiration, and therefore their shaping, from below. A positive attitude from the hierarchy is helpful, encouragement even more so. Whatever support is given should be a response to what is emerging and not a program for its emergence.

The sort of formation that clerics have received has not included the experience of living in an intentional community. Guidance and leadership for grassroots communities can only come out of those communities. Priests whose leadership instincts were socialized in most seminary contexts, and later in most parish and diocesan contexts, are not prepared to generate grassroots intentional communities. That is not their fault; it is just a matter of systemic change in how lay Christians gather.

Because religious women and men have been socialized in some of the instincts required for community living, they have often been more useful as resources for intentional community. Even so, religious do not, by and large, have the experience of grassroots efforts at constituting community; they have inherited models. In fact, Aylward Shorter reports that the permanent presence of religious men and women in African communities has sometimes tended to stifle local leadership.[6] The East African churches recognize these challenges, and are making serious efforts to respond to people's felt needs, and not impose their own plans.

While the SCC movement flourishes most in Eastern Africa, SCCs exist throughout the continent. In 1976, a synod of bishops of Rwandi and Burundi, in Central Africa, chose building communities as a theme and made a five-year plan. In Western Africa, the bishops of Upper Volta made SCCs the topic of their Easter meeting. In their judgment, SCC is the best way of inviting individual lay Christians to feel truly responsible for the life of the church, and to feel towards it as towards their family (i.e., to have characteristics of the primary group). There is much less SCC movement in South Africa. In March, 1985, nine bishops from South Africa went together on a study tour of SCCs in Zambia where they met with groups and with their leaders and then met among themselves. It remains to be seen what might happen in South Africa. The volatile political situation there could suggest a model closer to the BCCs of Latin America.

There are major differences, then, between the BCCs of Latin America and the SCCs of Africa.[7] BCCs are more of a grassroots initiative and find their *raison d'etre* in liberation themes, while SCCs are promoted from above and from the pastoral priorities felt there. SCCs, therefore, are predictably less politicized. As in the BCCs, shared prayer and mutual support are part of their commitment, but the transformation of society is less apt to be a conscious intention. In both areas, however, the small intentional communities experience themselves as a way of being church, and not as an activity of already existing churches.

The Philippines

In the Philippines the intentional Christian community is a serious commitment. The bishops of 75 Philippine dioceses have named the intentional community movement as their top pastoral priority. However, a survey conducted by a Jesuit sociologist indicates a diversity of understandings of the nature of these small communities.[8] The study discloses five different understandings on a continuum between conservative (ICCs function in existing church organization for the support of private spirituality) and liberal (a new form of church passionately concerned about both spirituality and the social problems of the world). The study also suggests that bishops are moving towards the latter understanding.

Because the model developed in the Philippine experience may be more relevant to North American needs, we will look closely at the experience of the diocese of Tagum.[9] There are 2,000 units in nearly 30 parishes, each of which includes 30 to 50 families. The primary group characteristics, therefore, are less pronounced. The community units select their own leadership and determine their own priorities. They do not initiate programs they cannot themselves afford and implement. These communities gather weekly for a Sunday liturgy of the Word and communion service. They also meet weekly for prayer and/ or for sharing experience. They have input sessions or seminars twice a year. Most of these communities have a Eucharist at least five times a year with a priest presider (there are just over 50 priests and three bishops for these communities).

Individual communities are gathered into "zones," each of which comprises five to 15 units. In this ecclesiology, the smaller units build *up* into larger units, rather than larger units that break *down* into smaller units. Each zone elects a president. The leaders of all the communities in a zone meet monthly, but they are not a decision-making body. Their meeting is a forum for sharing information. Also, and importantly, it is a ritual expression of the networked character of the small communities. The zone presidents constitute the Parish Council for the geographical parish unit to which they belong. The council and the priest are a decision-making body.

While leaders and ministers come up from below, all of them are required to receive systematic formation before their official installation as leader or minister. Formation for everyone includes basics on faith, an understanding of the small Christian community movement and its ecclesiology, scripture, and human relations. There are also specific programs for individual needs, such as homiletics, organization and management, accounting, and liturgical music.

Although the Philippines are a small area of the Christian world, we have paid particular attention to their experience because the church here seems to have found some ways of bridging both the African and Latin American experience by providing institutional support for grassroots efforts. We think this model may also come closer to a working model for the church in the United States.

Europe

Unlike Africa and Latin America, the house church communities in Europe are not a rural phenomenon. ICCs have sprung up and become networked in many of the countries of Western Europe. It is far more difficult to generalize the ICC movement in Europe than in Latin America. Social concern and social protest characterize many of the ICCs. Members of these communities are more apt to be middle-class Christians who have social concern and often engage in social protest. However, the ICCs in France have also been opened to the marginated peoples themselves. French ICCs are frequently on the edge of the institutional church and are sometimes (though not always) in opposition to it. The shortage of priests in France may galvanize the laity to assume more grassroots responsibility (of the 38,000 parishes in France, only 16,000 have full-time resident priest pastors); but so far that has not happened in any large way. In 1977, 340 delegates from 80 French ICCs met in Chamerolles. The cohesiveness of these groups is increasing through their networking.

In many other countries of Western Europe the ICCs are also making themselves felt. They exist in Belgium (especially in Hasselt and Bruges), Germany, and Switzerland. In Holland some of the ICCs have networked to form the *Nederlandse Basisbeweging*, or "Dutch Organization of Basic Communities." These communities have stayed in touch with the bishops. In Italy, the ICCs are more in evidence in the areas that are economically disadvantaged. In some places there has been uneasiness among the hierarchy. In Milan 16 ICCs lost their priest member as a result of disciplinary measures. However, the movement received clear support from the church at the "National Evangelizzonione e Promozione Humana" congress in 1976. In 1979, Bishop Onisto of Vincenza proposed a three-year pastoral program based upon the small intentional communities.

Let us look more closely now at Spain, the European country where the ICC movement is the most flourishing. Spanish interest in the ICCs is certainly related to Spain's longtime connections with the church of South America. At the 23rd Assembly of Spanish Bishops, Cardinal Tarancon of Madrid said, "We must first of all recognize that the splendid blossoming of Christian communities is not exclusive to our local church, nor does it come about through spontaneous generation: the Spirit wishes to tell us something. I think that we are faced with one of the signs of the times, and it is quite natural that we should try to decipher it." Even so, there have been problems between the communities and the hierarchy. Just a few years ago in the diocese of Almeria, six priests made a study of small catechumenate communities which they presented to Bishop Herras, who then abolished the communities. There was a fear of growing independence and idiosyncracy.[10] The potential idiosyncracy of ICCs is, indeed, a real danger. It plagued the small communities in Corinth. The "safety features" are in their networking and/or active dialogue with the institutional church.

In 1979 there was a meeting in Madrid, with 700 participants, called a "Meeting of Christians in Madrid for a Church of Liberation." The participants acknowledged their fear of negative response to the ICCs from a conservative hierarchy, and they set up structures for effective communication. The same year 1,200 people (half of them community leaders) participated in the "Fourth National Assembly of Christian Popular Communities" in Vallodolid. To help foster networking and internal communication, *Alander*, a monthly periodical for ICCs was founded in 1983. Its stated intention is worth quoting at length:

> We are engaged in building up an evangelical, dynamic community, which has a brotherly and egalitarian spirit, is pluralistic and liberating, ready to serve the most destitute and marginalized people. In this perspective we support socio-political projects in favor of justice, freedom, the defense of human rights, and solidarity among peoples. We wish to be an expression of a church which lives and acts in the perspectives and dynamics of Vatican II, taking into account the signs of the times.[11]

In a strange sort of way, the language of this statement both bristles with controversy (words like "egalitarian," "pluralistic," "socio-political projects") and at the same time evokes quite centrist sympathies in its defense of basic human rights and responsiveness to Vatican II. Having seen both battles and collaboration between the ICC movement and the hierarchical church, we might remember that social transformation is never painless. When a tested experience of [ecclesial] order vies with a possible [ecclesial] transmutation of order, lively tension is normal. In that situation, extensive listening of the old and new to each other is the only *redemptive* comportment possible.

Intentional Christian Communities within Our American Story

Just as house churches are different in different parts of Africa, so too are they different in different parts of the American continents. In the United States we are accustomed to calling ourselves "Americans" as if that were interchangeable with "United States citizens." The international press as well sometimes follows that usage. However, we want to acknowledge that the United States experience is but one version of the American story, therefore, we are going to be looking at the house church movement as it unfolds in *our* American story, not in *the* American story. Whenever we do speak of "American" in this context, we clearly mean only our own version.

The last 20 years witness to quite drastic developments in the Catholic church in the United States. Many of these transformations are responses to the Second Vatican Council, of course. But many of them also are responses to peculiarly Catholic history in this country independent of the council. Especially important, for example, is the upward mobility of Catholics educationally, intellectually, and socially.

Let us examine first some of the developments that are most clearly related to the Council, understanding of course that the U.S. "Americanness" of their setting is also a conditioning and causal factor.

Factually, statistics that mark the decrease in religious and priestly vocations are both stunning and sobering. The external manifestations hint at the deeper transformations of religious imagination among Catholics. There are fewer and fewer vocations to the priesthood and to religious life. Many fewer people are preparing themselves for the modes of church presence and ministry that have been the familiar mainstay of Catholic life.

The United States Catholic Conference sponsored *Research on Men's Vocations to the Priesthood and the Religious Life*, the results of which were published in 1984.[12] Some of the data in this report came from CARA studies.[13] Some of the data and projections also came from the Schoenherr-Sorenson Report,[14] published in 1981, and recently updated because of continuing observation of trends.[15] The numerical highpoint in religious and priestly vocations in the United States was the mid- and late '60s. In 1965 there were 8,885 seminarians for the diocesan priesthood, and in 1983 there were 3,821. During the same period the number of novices in men's clerical orders dropped from 3,000 to 642. In 1967 there were 1,008 ordinations to the priesthood. A projection based upon current enrollment suggests that in 1986 there will be 383 ordinations. The average age of priests and religious mounts. The 1970 high of about 37,000 diocesan priests in the United States is dwindling downwards. The earlier Schoenherr projections placed the optimistic estimate at 23,000 diocesan priests in the year 2000, the moderate estimate at 18,000, and the pessimistic estimate at about 13,000. His most recent projections are downward, with 14,000 or 15,000 being the moderate estimate. However, between 1965 and the year 2000, the American population will have increased about 38 percent. Already, three percent of American parishes are without a priest pastor, and that figure will mount very quickly. As I indicated earlier, of the 38,000 parishes in France, only about 16,000 have a resident priest pastor. There is no reason to think that the situation in the United States will be drastically different. No one, of course, can make guesses at what will be happening 50 or 75 years from now. Yet there is no realistic basis for believing that anything will change these predictions for the year 2000 in any substantial way (we are not that far away!).

Whether this information is good news or bad news is still another question. While the pain of these transformations is sometimes acute, it is our conviction that they are more like labor pains than the death rattle: the church of the People of God is being re-invented, that is, re-sourced in some of the deeper of its originating intuitions in Jesus Christ and the New Testament communities which proclaimed him the Christ. We are convinced that we are facing good news.

It is not as if this decline in priestly and religious vocations is leaving the church in this country bereft of leadership and ministry. Many new things are happening! The re-institution of the permanent diaconate is a new experiment in contemporary ministry (although its success in this country varies from region to region). The theology of the permanent diaconate is without reference to marriage. Church law allows for married deacons, though if a deacon's wife dies he may not remarry. A single deacon may not marry. But in fact well over 90 percent of permanent deacons in this country are married, and *their* report is that their marriages are constructively crucial to their sense of themselves as deacons, and they readily speak of "deacon wives" and "deacon families," an experience which diaconal theology has yet to assimilate. But for the first time in a very long time in the Roman church, married persons (men) have official ministries in the church.

The Notre Dame Study of parish life, released in 1985, indicates that beyond the priest pastor, 83 percent of church leadership and ministry in this country is lay (most of them volunteers). Moreover, parishes express satisfaction with and trust in these lay women and men. Increasingly, lay individuals and lay teams are preparing themselves professionally to serve as parish administrators. These pastoral agents are called "parish administrators" rather than "lay pastors" because canon law reserves "pastor" as a designation for the ordained community leader. Functionally, however, they are pastors. The new Code of Canon Law moves beyond what even Vatican II foresaw, acknowledging that lay members of Christ's faithful can participate in the church's jurisdictional power (129.2). Lay persons can also share in the exercise of pastoral care in a parish — not just minister, but share *in the exercise of pastoral care* (517.2). Lay people can also be leaders in the liturgy of the word, preside over liturgical prayer, confer baptism and distribute Holy Communion (230.3). They can preach in certain circumstances (766) and can assist at the sacrament of Marriage (1112.1).

To put it negatively, what lay "pastors" cannot be is the minister of the sacraments of eucharist, reconciliation, and anointing. However, as the Notre Dame Study points out, "arrangements for absentee pastors who provide the sacraments must not be considered a permanently accepted solution . . . priests are not likely to find this satisfying any more than parishioners do." What the solution will be is far from clear.

According to the Notre Dame study, lay leaders and ministers are usually longtime parishioners. They are from among the better-educated members of a parish. They are active people. About a fourth of them take part in four or more parish activities. Religiously and politically they tend to be close to the center. There are few from the far left or right who enter into parish ministries. The study indicates that these people are very generous and responsive. They easily do what is asked of them, but they are less likely to be initiators (which may be a result of their centrism).

The larger picture is both clear and hopeful: Christian people generally are assuming considerable responsibility for the life of their communities, and they are doing so competently.

We have already suggested (in the first chapter) some changes in religious imagination of the church and the return of its direction to the broader counsels of its people (and a hierarchy deeply puzzled over how it shall respect those broader counsels stemming from the faith experience of its people). We have never sat down to think out the inexorable logic of the People of God metaphor. And if we had, we almost certainly would not have predicted the church of the final years of the second millennium that is making its appearance. Once we said "Yes" to the "People of God" as a new root metaphor, it began to work its own inexorable logic upon us, that of art and not that of rational reflection. It has been constructing a new narrative. Our symbols often know so much more about us than we know about them.

As we also indicated in the first chapter, it is a very old and revered Western Christian understanding that marks ontological differences between worldly and religious, between temporal and non-temporal, between profane and sacred. Such an imagination gives priests primary responsibility for the sacred order, and laity for the temporal order. If one contemporary "problem" of priests and religious is that their active participation in politics (the "temporal" order) violates the two-world view, the "problem" of laity doing priestly things marks their forced entry into responsibility for the sacred order. What was breaking down already in *The Church and the Modern World* is continuing to express itself as an operative transformation of the religious imagination. It is the fuller historicization of God's redemptive presence. History is where we are and is the only place we have for meeting God. Because God is there to be met, it is sacred history. Alfred North Whitehead once remarked that God is in the world or nowhere.[15] For us that is certainly true: the world is where *we* are, and we can only meet what is there in the world with us and related to us.

Post-conciliar American Catholics share in the re-direction of spiritual energy to the transformation of historical experience that Vatican II spawned. Politicized priests and ecclesialized lay persons witness together to a religious imagination rooted in a one-world vision. The intricacies of the new dispensation slowly work themselves out. Both tendencies come under the critical scrutiny of the older world view, as current tiffs between Cardinals Ratzinger and Hamer on the one side, and theologians Schillebeeckx, Boff, and Segundo on thee other exemplify.

In a recent publication, *American Catholics Since the Council: An Unauthorized Report*, Andrew Greeley provides some further information about American Catholics.[16] A sociological change important in the evolution of American Catholicism is the professional and economic advancement of Catholics. For example, in 1966 25 percent of collegians in this country were Catholic; in 1985 45 percent were Catholic. In the early '60s, Catholics and Protestants were economically and occupationally about on a par; by 1985 Catholics, on the average, had moved ahead of Protestants in these same respects.

Greeley reports that while there was a drop in church membership during the late '60s and '70s among Catholics, that has leveled off. In 1970, 15 percent of those born Catholic had left the church, and this figure was exactly the same in 1985. Although Catholicity may express itself in a variety of ways, Greeley notes that an incredible loyalty to Catholic identity continues to obtain among Catholics.

The increased educational and economic status has generated a more independent Catholic, and the controversy over *Humanae Vitae* was a watershed in the development of that independence. There are Catholics who disagree with church teaching on birth control and have left the church. There are Catholics within the church who agree with the teaching. However, Greeley's studies show that the number of Catholics who disagree with the teaching but remain sacramentally active in the church is larger than the other two groups combined. Nor is it as though Catholics have elected to disregard all church teaching. The effect of the American bishops' pastoral, *The Challenge of Peace*, has been both extraordinary and unexpected. In a survey taken in 1983, Greeley notes that 34 percent of both Catholics and Protestants thought that the United States spent too much money on the arms race. A year after the pastoral, 54 percent of Catholics felt we overspend on arms, while the figure remained at 34 percent for Protestants. The bishops' pastoral appears to have had a profound effect upon the positions of individual Catholics. This seems to indicate that Catholics do listen to official instruction, but today they tend to respond independently and critically from their own experience. We suspect that their move from national ghettos (the Italian, Polish, or Irish parish) to the mainstream American ethos may well be one causative factor in this phenomenon.

The Greeley study shows that Catholics tend to stand politically with the Democrats. The last two elections are not enough to indicate a long-term trend in another direction. No matter how Catholics identify their political affiliation, three-fifths of them vote Democratic in congressional and senatorial elections. Catholics, Greeley reports, are substantially more liberal on the average than are Protestants, though to be sure there are politically and religiously conservative Catholics. The National Opinion Research Center reports that over the past four decades American Catholics moved faster on racial issues than Protestants in the same geographical area. Catholics took a stand against the Vietnam War before the typical American did, and Catholics give large support to the nuclear freeze. On the issue of gun control, support comes from 57 percent of Protestants, 82 percent of Catholics, and 96 percent of Jews. In summary, Greeley says that on just about every measure of social attitudes, Catholics occupy a middle position between Jews and Protestants, a bit left of center.

Against this background, we look at the intentional Christian community movement in this country. What the movement in the world shares, in spite of many cultural differences, is a commitment to making human life qualitatively safer, stronger, lovelier, and more gracious; that is, to cooperate with God in the creation of a New Earth. We want a safe world, where we readily allow each other into our lives. We want to know how we can build into our communities the qualities of trust, support, and mutuality that encourage us to allow each other a significant role in our identity formation. And we want that interaction to be subject to constant critique so that our life together grows in its ability to empower us all. We also have a mobilized concern for what goes on in the larger world around us. Those large systems must be the subject of transformation and conversion every bit as much as our individual lives and our smaller communities.

In situations we have examined, the small Christian communities often form among those people who, when organized and networked, gain the power to effect social transformation. In Latin America, where there is a smaller and less effective middle-class base, the communities are found among the poor and disenfranchised. In the United States, it is the large middle class which, when effectively conscientized, is able to put our culture under requirement for social transformation, as the peace and racial justice movements have demonstrated.

While these goals are shared with many secular humanists, the intentional Christian community movement finds itself rooted as well in its faith in a God whose redemptive work in the world expresses itself in the continual prophetic call to creative transformation. As Joe Holland notes, this small community movement brings together the two seeds of creativity: social engagement and spirituality.[17] When Schillebeeckx was asked about prayer in a published interview, he remarked that prayer without social engagement is reduced to mere sentimentality, while political activity without prayer often becomes grim and even barbaric.[18]

It is difficult to get an accurate reading on the extensiveness of ICCs in the United States. What is certain is that the movement is well underway. What is highly probable is that it will grow considerably in the next decade. What is vital is that there be an indigenously American appropriation of this movement. We must use our own best resources to address our own deepest needs.

A Jesuit Woodstock study of a selected group of house churches in the United States has been published as *Tracing the Spirit*.[19] The study focuses, for the most part, upon groups in the vicinity of Washington, D.C. The Center for Concern in Washington, D.C. organized a communication network for these small groups, The American Catholic Lay Network (ACLN), and began collecting data on groups of ICCs functioning in the United States. The response justified making ACLN a separate operation. A quarterly newsletter for small communities, *Gathering*, was founded by the *National Catholic Reporter*, and is now published under the auspices of the ACLN.[20] The National Federation for Priests' Councils set up a special commission out of its national office in Chicago to address the small community movement in this country, and has published two manuals now to help facilitate the ICC movement.[21] U.S. American interest in intentional Christian communities is growing quickly.

The Woodstock study guesses that in 1979 there were 15,000 ICCs in the United States. Their number has grown considerably since then. Groups that are not originally ICCs, lacking either the mutuality of the primary group or the mission/external concern of the secondary group, sometimes become ICCs. For example, Renew groups in the parishes are brought together for specific periods of time and specific purposes: to understand better and appropriate more deeply the many forms of post-conciliar renewal. However, as Joseph Champlin reports for the Syracuse area, "swift bonding, mutual care and reaching out . . . happened in many, if not most, groups."[22] (As Renew got underway in Syracuse, 20,000 people belonged to about 2,000 small groups.) The archdiocese of Newark was the first to establish a special department for Small Communities (directed by Sr. Catherine Nerney) within its Office of the Ministry of Leadership Development, mostly as a response to Renew Groups that wanted to continue after their formal program had been completed. Paulist Press has published a number of fascicles of the Pilgrimage series, a series of texts that has come from the Newark archdiocese, designed to guide the formation of ICCs, and to facilitate their *leitouriga* of the Word in small communities.[23]

Carole Eipers reports a similar phenomenon in Chicago. Groups that did not begin with secondary group characteristics add to their original intentions on-going concern for single parents, or for the homebound, or peace and justice concerns.[24] This is an increasingly common occurrence for groups that were not originally intentioned as ICCs, but later develop in that direction, e.g., Marriage Encounter, Cursillo, Prayer Groups, Peace and Social Justice groups. It may be a matter of adding organized and implemented social concern to a prayer group, or of adding interpersonal concerns and mutual support to a nuclear freeze group. Some ICCs, of course, are not developments out of other groups. In the Boston area, for example, dozens of small groups are flourishing.[25] Some of these are supported by Jesuits (in and around Weston) and Paulists (Beacon Hill). It is not uncommon to find ICC groups spawned by Catholic colleges and universities, especially those which have institutional connections with religious orders. In the Boston area there are campus ICC groups at Boston College, Boston University, Harvard, and M.I.T.

John Langan reports upon some of the characteristics of ICCs in the United States:

Thus, if one may venture a general sketch of these groups, their members are above average in education without being professional academics or intellectuals: they belong to the post-1945 suburban phase of U.S. church history rather than to immigrant nationality groups. They are predominantly white and middle class, inclined to frugality and generosity rather than to conspicuous consumption. They are disinclined to violence but prize order and security. They are democratic and egalitarian but not rebellious or anarchist by disposition. The central members of these groups, who may or may not be in positions of leadership at any given time, are articulate and are accustomed to stating and resolving the issues of their lives on their own terms. Most of the groups described themselves and their members as ranging from center and slightly left of center to the far left on the contemporary spectrum of political ideology. As a consequence, issues of power are often central for these groups. The groups and their members are anxious to preserve their autonomy in the face of larger religious and social units. They are likely to be uneasy about the unequal distribution of power within the group, and they are drawn to conceive of the empowerment of people (both their own members and their clients) as a characteristic contribution of the group.[26]

We must remember, of course, that this is a generalization from the particular groups investigated by the Woodstock team. On the whole, the description seems valid for white, middle-class persons, who constitute the majority of U.S. Catholics, many of whom are forming ICCs. However, a very significant and increasingly large U.S. Catholic minority is Hispanic. There are indeed ICCs among Hispanics, and these tend to reflect the Latin American model, though even racial minorities in the U.S. are not untouched by the values of the American cultural ethos. There are Hispanic ICCs in a number of areas, e.g., San Francisco, Santa Fe (with encouragement from Archbishop Roberto

Sanchez), and San Antonio (where there is currently some fear of meeting because agents from the Immigration and Naturalization Service sometimes appear, too).

As we have tried to say in many different ways, the growing number of small, intentional Christian communities are not simply helpful groups springing up to meet special needs — though they are that, too. There is a good chance that the house churches, an old idea, are inventing a new way of being church in the final decades of the second millennium. They are not counter-hierarchical. They do not experience themselves as eccentric or peripheral, but as basic instances of ecclesial existence.

They are countercultural, but not like the communes of Berkeley and San Francisco a couple of decades ago. Those communes withdrew and established alternative lifestyles. Today's house churches are in the mainstream. However, in many ways they are deeply countercultural as they work for social reconstructions that are more deeply faithful to the sisterhood and brotherhood of all human beings. The parenthood of God, the moment it is experienced, suffuses itself into the nooks and crannies of every relational system. The Body of Christ and the body politic are not identical, but they are inextricably and internally related.

The ICCs are not a uniform movement, precisely because they reflect the plurality of cultures in which they arise. Therefore our indigenously American house churches cannot but disclose features of their U.S. origination. If these house churches are to be transformative of their own cultural milieu, they must engage themselves in those parts of our American deep story most in need of transformation, just as they must also celebrate those achievements of our American mythos that are most deeply consonant with the Judaeo-Christian deep story. We must turn, then, to our American story as a setting for the ICC to see what kind of house churches we might hope to see raised "from California to the New York Island, from the redwood forests to the gulfstream waters."

SUGGESTED READINGS

Theology for Intentional Christian Communities

The ICC movement extends far beyond the Latin American experience. Latin America, however, is the place where the experiment is both the most extensive and the best reflected upon. Although many adaptations must be made for the American situation, the theological reflection of Latin America is extremely rich, helpful and hopeful. The literature is vast. We offer a few select recommendations. There is no better place to begin than the two general conferences of Latin American Bishops, first at Medellin and than at Puebla. The pastoral recommendations of Medellin ask "that a greater number of eccesial communities be formed in the parishes, particularly in rural and marginal areas." Consonant with the suggestion of the Whiteheads that true Christian community is a hybrid of both primary and secondary group characteristics, Medellin recognizes that the base community will develop "to a degree that its members have a sense of belonging [primary] that leads them to solidarity in a common mission [secondary], and accomplishment of common active participation, conscientious and fruitful, in liturgical and community living" (6.13). The conclusions of the 1968 Medellin Conference are published as *The Church in the Present-Day Transformation of Latin America in the Light of the Council* (Washington, D.C.: Secretariat for Latin America, NCCB, 1979). At Puebla the Latin American Bishops picked up the theme of "The Evangelization of Culture" made so clearly in Paul VI's *Evangelii Nuntiandi*. Section two of Chapter II is especially recommended, "The Evangelization of Culture." *Mutatis mutandis*, the house churches in North American culture can profit from the lived experience of the Latin churches. The conclusions of the Puebla Conference are published as *Puebla: Evangelization at Present and in the Future of Latin America* (Washington, D.C.: Secretariat, Committee for the Church in Latin America, NCCB, 1979). One must remember, however, in reading these two documents that they are hierarchical discussions (though indeed supportive) of what is basically a grass roots movement. For voices closer to the movement, see the collection of essays, Sergio Torres and John Eagleson, editors, *The Challenge of Basic Christian Communities* (Maryknoll: Orbis, 1981), especially chapters 8-16 which constitute Part II, "Reflections on Popular Christian Communities." If you were to pick but one book to read, you wouldn't go wrong with Leonardo Boff's *Ecclesiogenesis: The Base Communities Reinvent the Church* (Maryknoll: Orbis, 1986). Especially noteworthy is Boff's strong theological rationale for the true ecclesial reality of basic Christian communities.

The Latin American Church: Further Descriptions

For the interested reader, several other very helpful texts can be mentioned: Alvaro Barreiro, *Basic Ecclesial Communities: The Evangelization of the Poor* (Maryknoll: Orbis, 1982); Michel Bavarel, *New Communities, New Ministries: The Church Resurgent in Latin America* (Maryknoll: Orbis, 1984); William R Burrows, *New Ministries: The Global Context* (Maryknoll: Orbis, 1980).

The American Scene

Our three recommendations have already been cited in the chapter. *Gathering: The Small Group Newsletter*, is published bi-monthly by the National Catholic Lay Network, P.O. Box 42559, Washington, D.C. 20015-0559. This popular style periodical regularly carries information on small communities in the American church. Evelyn and James Whitehead's *Community of Faith: Models and Strategies for Developing Christian Communities* (N.Y.: Seabury, 1982) speaks the language that Americans increasingly find helpful: it integrates much material from the human sciences, and provides language that can help any small community reflect on its dynamics. The great advantage of James Hug's (editor) *Tracing the Spirit* (N.Y.: Paulist, 1983) is its phenomenological approach. Its conclusions are based upon interviews with members of 16 different communities. As valuable as is the report it offers upon community experience, it is also an excellent example of theological reflection in the mode of "praxis." It is a sustained conversation between contemporary experience and the church's story. The whole book, in a sense, is an example of how any house church might fruitfully reflect upon its experience. In this regard, we especially recommend Thomas E. Clarke's chapter 1, "A New Way: Reflecting on Experience," and Larry Rasmussen's chapter 12, "Community Reflection." The book's limitation, of course, is its very narrow data base. All the communities examined are near Washington, D.C. Yet it is a model for how it reflects upon the experience at its disposal.

Notes

1. Evelyn Eaton Whitehead and James D. Whitehead, *Community of Faith* (N.Y.: Seabury, 1982), chapters 2 and 3, esp. pp. 26-28, and the very helpful chart on p. 45.

2. Leonardo Boff, *Ecclesiogenesis: The Base Communities Reinvent the Church* (Maryknoll: Orbis, 1986), esp. chapter 3.

3. *Pro Mundi Vita: Ministries and Communities*, a trimestrial publication out of Brussels, is probably the best resource for tracking with the experience of the larger church in these two areas. References to this periodical will be to *PMV*.

4. *PMV*, (43) 1985/1, pp. 2-6.

5. *PMV*, (41) 1983/3, pp. 5-9.

6. Aylward Shorter, "Small Christian Communities in Eastern Africa," *Maryknoll's World Apostolate Bulletin* (25), July-August, 1985/227.

7. *PMV*, (41) 1983/3, pp.2-5.

8. *PMV*, (42) 1984/4. pp. 9-11.

9. *PMV*, (45) 1985/3, pp. 14-18.

10. *PMV* (38) 1983/4, p. 3.

11. *PMV*, (38) 1983/4, p. 3.

12. Dean R. Hoge, et. al, *Research on Men's Vocations to the Priesthood and Religious Life* (Washington, D.C.: United States Catholic Conference, 1984).

13. *Catholic Institutions for the Training of Candidates for the Priesthood* (Washington, D.C.: Center for Applied Research for the Training of Candidates for the Priesthood, 1979).

14. Richard Schoenherr and Annamette Sorenson, "Decline and Change in the U.S. Catholic Church from the Second Vatican Council to the Second Millenium," *Correspondent Report No. 5* (Madison: Univ. of Wisconsin, 1981). This study has since been updated based upon a continuing evaluation of data and trends, indicating that the 1981 projections for the year 2000 must be lowered. The more recent projections for the number of active ordained priests for 2000 is about 15,000, compared with the 37,000 at the peak in the late 1960s. In that earlier period, the number of priests 55 and older comprised about 25 percent on the total. In 2000, Schoenherr projects, they will comprise 50 percent of the total.

15. Alfred North Whitehead, *The Dialogues of Alfred North Whitehead*, ed. Lucien Price (Boston: Little, Brown, and Co., 1954), pp.370-371.

16. Andrew Greeley, *American Catholics Since the Council: An Unauthorized Report* (Chicago: Thomas More, 1985).

17. Joe Holland and Peter Henriot, *Social Analysis: Linking Faith and Justice* (Maryknoll: Orbis, 1983, 2nd ed.), p. xiv.

18. Edward Schillebeeckx, *God Is New in Each Moment* (NY: Seabury, 1983), p. 124.

19. James Hug, ed., *Tracing the Spirit* (NY: Paulist, 1983).

20. *Gathering* is a small group newsletter published bi-monthly which addresses the small community movement in the United States. It was originally published under the auspices of *National Catholic Reporter's* Sheed & Ward, but is now published by the American Catholic Lay Network in Washington, D.C. This is the best current medium for tracking with the intentional Christian community movement in the United States. In addition to articles on particular communities and experiments, there are theological discussions, and theoretical and pastoral articles.

21. *Developing Basic Christian Communities: A Handbook* (1979), and *Basic Christian Communities: The United States Experience* (no date), both published under the auspices of the National Federation of Priests' Councils, Chicago.

22. Joseph Champlin, "Bonding through Renew Small Groups," *Gathering*, Sept.-Oct. 1985/4, pp. 1-2.

23. Catherine Nerney, *Called to Be Faithful* (N.Y.: Paulist, 1985), *Enrollment in the School of Discipleship* (also Paulist, 1983), *The Experience of Lent with the Risen Christ* (also Paulist, 1983) are all helpful guides for small community reflection upon scripture. The entire pilgrimage series is very useful for small groups who want to reflect together either as house church communities, or as groups interested in moving towards community life. In the latter regard, we note Thomas Kleissler, Joseph Slinger and Catherine Martin, *Moving Toward Small Christian Communities: An Ongoing Model of Parish Life* (N.Y.: Paulist, 1983).

24. Carole Eipers, "Chicago: Small Groups and Social Action," *Gathering*, Nov.-Dec. 1985/5, p. 3.

25. *PMV*, (45) 1985/3, pp. 11-15.

26. John Langan, "Models and Values: The Search for U.S. Christian Community," in *Tracing the Spirit*, p. 161.

Chapter 3

U.S. CULTURE AND CHRISTIAN COMMUNITIES

Individualism and Community
in the United States

After surveying the movement of small Christian communities in some of its major cultural expressions across the face of the earth, we noted its emergence in the culture of the United States of America. Now we shall address that culture more closely. In some ways our culture evokes a hunger for community: our loneliness as individuals can be quite profound. In other ways our American way of life can militate strongly against community: American individualism can be singularly asocial. Individual dignity and freedom are held sacred in our culture. Can such individuals find a less disconnected way of being together without giving up personal dignity and freedom? Put religiously, the question is: can we redeem our precious individuality by transforming it into a radically relational form?

An aphorism of psychotherapist Fritz Perls, which became a popular poster, hints at our current dilemma:

> You do your thing and I do mine. I am not in this
> world to live up to your expectations, and you are not
> here to live up to mine. You are you and I am I and if
> by chance we find each other, it's beautiful; if not, it
> can't be helped.

Our advertising images of admirable people — the Marlboro
man, the individual entrepreneur, the career achievers who
have always known just who they are — also hold important
clues about the contemporary cultural world of the United
States.[1] How can a Marlboro man become a candidate for intentional community?

As a bright and articulate young woman wrote recently in an
essay entitled "The value of my American citizenship": "To live
a life chosen and controlled exclusively by myself is essential to
my happiness and dignity. Because America offers this opportunity, it is the quintessence of freedom.[2]." Or as a well-known behavioral scientist recently put the point: "Happiness is having
the maximum number of personal choices ahead of you," and
again, "Success is living the kind of life you want to—no matter
what that is."[3]

Such statements are never "just words." Words are language,
and language is the house we live in as human beings. Language
has a quasi-religious character, in fact, because it reflects our
preconscious sense of what is "really real." To talk in the kind of
language just quoted is to live in a world where the experiences,
rights and choices of individuals are presumed to be the center-
piece of life. Everything else, including society, culture and even
our planet itself, stands in danger of becoming merely a means
to life's ultimate goal of individual fulfillment.

Our cultural individualism inevitably shapes our American
language; the individualistic words and phrases that abound in
our everyday talk shape our American way of life. And so it goes,
in a self-perpetuating cycle. As we will see, such talk reflects the
primary web of cultural meanings out of which our lives as

American persons and as a people are currently being fashioned.

The American individualism so characteristic of the contemporary United States generates a pervasive loneliness and anxiety.[4] Such feelings in turn create a hunger for integrating experiences of solidarity. But precisely as individualists, we are predictably ambivalent about relational commitments. This leaves us in a massive cultural "double bind" that tends to drive us crazy or call forth change.[5] If our cultural individualism works against community, our collective hunger for more solid connections — however ambivalent and muted in its expression — is an opening in our culture for new possibilities of communal commitment. This is the redeeming gift that intentional Christian communities have to offer us: a way of social transformation that honors the sacredness of the individual.

There is a specific way, a redemptive way, that we might live together as individuals in the world. It is our hope that this book will help that way of life stand up as a compelling possibility before us who live, move and have our being within the culture of the U.S. We call that possibility the house church or intentional Christian community, and will develop a working model of what we mean by it in the next chapter. But since this text is primarily addressed to persons living in the cultural context of the United States of America, we must take the time now to explore what that version of being American is all about. For it is our profound conviction that small Christian communities within our culture cannot fail to be shaped by and contribute to the shape of the particular way of being human which has emerged in the culture of the United States.

What Is a Culture?

Since we are asking what the house church might look like when built with the U.S. version of cultural materials, it is important to get clear about what we mean by "culture." A culture is a particular way of living which is shared among a group of human beings. Its patterns provide coherence in the lives of its participants by orienting them toward a common set of meanings which give order and purpose to their existence. This set of collective meanings is inherited historically and passed on from generation to generation as long as a people survives. A culture's meanings are carried and transmitted in its symbols. Our cultures give form to the particular kinds of people we are.[6]

It is useful to think of culture as a web made up of three interconnected "sub-webs": a set of symbols, an ethos and a world view.

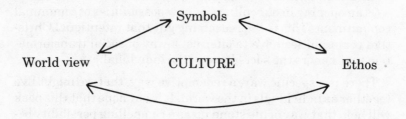

These are the three underlying and always interrelated dimensions of what we mean by "culture." Let's look at each in turn, before turning our attention to the particular symbols, world view and ethos of contemporary American culture.

Symbols

Symbols are grids or filters which give particular form to our experience. These symbolic sources of information are not genetic, but are located in the world of shared meanings called culture.[7] Within intentional Christian communities, our collective practices of *kerygma* and *leitourgia* carry the tradition's classical sacred symbols of baptism, cross, eucharist meal and so on.

As we become socialized into the particular symbolic world of a culture, we learn to experience in a specific, culturally informed way. Socialized human beings do not first have bare experiences and then add labels; we perceive everything as belonging to this or that cultural or symbolic category.[8] Culture continually gives shape to our perceptions, teaching us to interpret things in certain ways rather than others. Members of intentional Christian communities in the United States will be profoundly accustomed to our American way of perceiving, of making meaning. Our purpose in this chapter is to explore that way of making meaning.

The most pervasive and influential set of symbols within which we learn to live is our native language. Nothing shapes our experience of reality more potently. For example, in Maidu, a particular native American language, there are only three words available to describe the spectrum which English speakers call the "basic colors": "lak" (red), "tit" (green-blue) and "tulak" (yellow-orange-brown). Native speakers of a language with only three basic color terms will be aware of fewer distinctions in their experience of color; speakers with more color categories available in their language routinely make more distinctions within their experience of color. For example, with the same two objects in front of them an English speaker sees one yellow and one orange book, a Maidu speaker sees two "tulak" books.[9] In a similar vein, the native languages of certain Eskimo tribes have more than a dozen words available to describe various shades of snow, and native speakers of those languages seem to perceive and live with "snow" in more nuanced ways than native speakers of English. Everyone's language affects her or his experience in analogous ways.

Words are symbols, as are the particular rules of grammar, syntax and context by which its speakers combine smaller meaning units into larger ones. When we employ rule-governed sentences in various life settings, the linguistic rules have constant effects on how we experience those settings which are like the effects of the color words on English and Maidu experiencing. Our language and other symbols never merely describe "the facts" of our world, but are always contributing to our collective construction of what "the facts" are. Language is like a lens which shapes what will stand out in our experience and what will remain in the background. All human perception and understanding occur within the "symbolic medium of language.[10]

Languages contain narrative structures — story lines — which give direction to lives. Many commentators, for example, have noted how the Christian great story has become part of the "plot" of Western civilization, although that civilization has long since stopped understanding itself as "Christendom."[11] This point will be pursued further in our discussion of cultural world views.

To be creatures of language (and, therefore, of symbol) is to learn to experience reality in the symbolic forms characteristic of cultures. For creatures of culture — that is, for human beings — there are no uninterpreted facts. Anyone who has spent even a little while around an intentional Christian community will hear a different language about the individual than the Marlboro man speaks. House-church language is in certain important respects, countercultural to the mores of mainstream U.S. culture. But when these countercultural Christian communities are also part of that cultural context, they provide a way for a non-individualistic language to make its way into the deeper strains of our version of the American story.

World View
The patterns of meanings which we inherit linguistically are always carried in tales about how things in the universe began, how they are and ought to be, and how they will (or at least might) end. This picture of reality conveys the *world view* of a culture.[12] It may be a highly complex and analytical account of various levels of reality (e.g., sub-atomic, atomic, molecular, organic, etc.), complete with empirical evidence to support the analysis. The "Big Bang" is part of a story which conveys such a world view. Or it may be a fundamental division of reality into matter and spirit, arrived at through a revelation preserved in sacred, mythical stories. The creation accounts of many premodern cultures convey such a world view.[13]

We take our cultural world view for granted, and become conscious of it only when it fails to work in some practical situation or when it is confronted by someone else's different story about reality.[14] In our time such a confrontation is being played out in U.S. culture in the controversy between evolutionary and creationist interpretations of reality. This is a case of world views in conflict, and the intensity of feeling on both sides is a good clue to how important people's world views are to them. To challenge a world view is to upend the world people inhabit and take for granted.

In learning the language and other shared practices of our culture — a process which goes on from conception through death — we are always (and typically unconsciously) absorbing and internalizing a picture of how physical and social reality work. Whereas animals receive their pictures of how the world works principally through genetic information (e.g., how to construct a beehive) and relatively simple forms of learning, human beings live in worlds made out of meaning.[15] The plans for our projects — our beehives — reside not in our genes, but in our symbols, that is to say in our cultural heritages. These cultural blueprints undergo continual transformation as the human story unfolds in our ongoing historical movement from memory to expectation.

The world view of a people includes not just how things are in reality for them, but how they have been and might be. Cultures are communities of memory and expectation. A people's world view reflects both its awareness of history and its corporate expectations for the future. Any option for living which is inconsistent with our world view will not be experienced by us as possible unless and until it becomes consistent with our picture of how things are. For members of intentional Christian communities in any culture this is a crucial awareness. For members of such communities in America, this awareness reminds us that the Christian *kerygma* must be experienced as holding up a relevant and compelling set of possibilities in our American time and place.

Human beings are the creatures for which it is profoundly the case that any situation which is perceived as real will be real in its effects.[16] And the sum total of what we perceive as real is our world view, as embodied for us in our language and other symbol systems.

Ethos

Our language always carries reminders about how life has been and might be. It is also nuanced to remind us of how our lives ought to be lived, of ways of being human which are appropriate in the kind of world we inhabit. This shared image of the good life is the *ethos* of a culture.[17] Our word "ethics" comes from the same root. A people's ethos may dictate a highly detailed set of steps for the composition of our days (as, e.g., in certain professional and religious subcultures) or merely a general guideline or set of principles to be observed in pursuing our goals (e.g., "Treat others as you would like to be treated," or "Let's do it to them before they do it to us").

As we learn the language and otherwise become enculturated within our particular group over the course of a lifetime, we are always (and, once again, typically unconsciously) absorbing and internalizing a sense of how our lives ought to be lived if we are to be valued by the other participants in our cultural world — if we are to "belong." Our culture's ethos will serve us as a kind of taken-for-granted personal and social ethic for the conduct of our lives, unless and until it fails us or is challenged.

The ethos of *koinonia* and *diakonia* to which members of intentional Christian communities hold themselves accountable flows from the Christian *kerygma*: Christian social ethics reflect the Christian narrative.[18] Because the Christian great story is not identical with the American great story in certain very important respects, the ethos called for on the part of members of intentional Christian communities within U.S. culture will be complex and often countercultural.[19] Its narratives bear memories and raise possibilities that will be experienced as dangerous.

Having spoken of *koinonia, diakonia* and *kerygma* in the Christian ethos, it remains important to say something in this context about Christian *leitourgia.* An example is a good place to start. Both of the authors of this book were members of an intentional Christian community in Minnesota. Mike's four-year-old daughter, Katie, had a penchant for both raspberries and bubble gum. When Bernard saw some bubble gum in a store, shaped like little raspberries, he got it for her and gave it to her one Sunday morning after the community's eucharist. Several days later he asked her whether she had chewed all the gum. "I only chewed two," Katie said, "and I gave the others to my friends." "That was really beautiful, Katie," said Bernard. "Well," said Katie, "that's what we all do with the bread on Sunday." No one ever made that explicit connection for Katie. She had simply internalized the spirit she had felt within our intentional community's eucharistic *leitourgia,* and acted out of it in her own life in a very natural and concrete way.

One helpful way of understanding the ethos of a people is to focus on the moods and motivations typical of their shared style of life. By *moods* we mean underlying and formative feelings about life that pervade the experience of people in a culture.[20] This doesn't mean that every person in the cultural group will always feel a particular way, but that there is a tendency within the group to share a particular feeling response toward their existence. When we speak, for example, of American optimism we know very well that not every American is always optimistic, and yet this mood has seemed to many an apt description of one important feeling tone in the U.S. version of the American experience. The same can be said of British reserve or Irish romanticism: these are not descriptions of how everyone within these groups always feels, but of tendencies within the cultural groups to share particular feeling responses to life based on shared histories.

By *motivations* we refer to shared tendencies among members of a cultural group to behave in certain ways. As Americans, for example, we tend toward individualism ("I can take care of my-

self") and activism ("Let's get on with it ") in our collective motivations.[21] Once again, this does not mean that all Americans are
always individualistic or activistic in their motivations, but that
tendencies in those directions seem to be shared behavioral in-
clinations within our rendition of American life. What do you
think of as some of the classical motivations associated with the
Christian story?

As we observed in our discussion of world view, the ethos of a
people likewise has to do with their interpretation not only of
actuality, but also of possibility. How our life together might go
is influenced in very large ways by how we have "always" done
things. New possibilities for living must become gradually
rooted in the concrete and customary way of life of a people, if
they are to have a chance of becoming a significant and lasting
part of their cultural world. In order to have a vital and sustainable incarnation in the United States, then, the way of life called
intentional Christian community must come to terms with our
American ethos.[22] Such communities must mediate the dangerous memories of Christian tradition in this time and place; the
more vital the mediation, the larger its effect on our culture.

The world view and ethos of a cultural group are mutually
reinforcing. As Clifford Geertz has observed about religious
symbols:

> In religious belief and practice a group's ethos is rendered
> intellectually reasonable by being shown to represent a
> way of life ideally adapted to the actual state of affairs the
> world view describes, while the world view is rendered
> emotionally convincing by being presented as an image of
> an actual state of affairs peculiarly well-arranged to ac-
> commodate such a way of life.[23]

Although this reinforcement of ethos by world view and vice
versa is characteristic of all the realms of culture (education,
politics, business, etc.), it operates most strikingly in the realm
of sacred symbols of religion and nationhood.[24] Members of in-

tentional Christian communities attempt to incarnate the world view and ethos embedded in the Christian Great Story in their historical moment.

By living within and absorbing the meanings embodied in a culture's language and symbols, we become and remain a member of the group. We soak up, as if by osmosis, a view of how reality is structured and a correlative sense of the good life for human beings who find themselves within such a reality. The ethos and world view which are embodied in our culture's language and other symbols, and which is always in a process of transformation, will serve us as a continuously shifting life-long map, an ever-changing horizon for orienting our collective and personal existence from day to day. For the most part, the ongoing transformation of our cultural horizons is so gradual as to be imperceptible from day to day.

To exist within U.S. or Christian culture, or within both of them, is to share with others the meanings embodied in common sets of symbols, especially a common language. Sharing those meanings entails sharing a typical way of perceiving and thinking (world view) and a typical way of acting (ethos). Whether we know it or not, or are prepared to acknowledge it or not, even our cherished American individualism is an aspect of such cultural patterns. The individual who rejects particular aspects of her or his culture is still speaking and thinking in a language and thereby participating in culture. There is no place outside of culture for human beings to be.[25]

The extraordinary power of culture in our lives resides partly in the fact that we ordinarily take its most basic assumptions about reality and its guidelines for living entirely for granted. The world view and everyday way of life of our cultural group — our shared tendencies to perceive, think, feel, value and act in particular ways — become for us the "natural" way of being human. It is, as we have already noted, only when our taken-for-granted cultural map fails to work or is subject to radical challenge that we may be forced to step back from our accustomed pathways of thought, feeling, valuing and action, thereby becoming aware of other possibilities for human life in the world.

As human beings the question is not whether we operate symbolically within a particular world view and ethos. Everyone who speaks a language does so, because human beings always experience through the symbolic filters of our native cultures. The question, rather, is what world of meaning we inhabit and what particular mixture of light and shadow it sheds in front of our existence, what memories and possibilities it reveals to us and conceals from us as persons and as a people.

Human cultures are communities of memory and anticipation.[26] What we remember and what we expect are always deeply interrelated. Our shared interpretation of the settled past continually makes particular possibilities stand out against our future horizons while others remain occluded from our vision. This is one way of saying that our cultural web is "temporally thick," that human existence is always grounded within a particular past which is always projecting us toward particular futures. There is no culture without an already interpreted history, and no history which does not give rise to and limit possible futures. Whenever we retrieve or reinterpret aspects of our past, we simultaneously transform the futures on our horizon. Through our participation in culture, our past is always present in our present creation of the future. The memories and expectations of intentional Christian communities within our American culture always bear the mark of our American story, but they should never be limited solely to those particular memories and possibilities. Such communities also bear memories which challenge current arrangements and hopes which keep the image of one just and loving world on our horizon.

In the diagram at the beginning of this section, the arrows connecting the three "sub-webs" of culture go in both directions. Each arrow means "influences and is influenced by." Within every culture, then, symbols influence and are influenced by a world view which influences and is influenced by an ethos which influences and is influenced by symbols which influence and are influenced by a world view, and so on endlessly, web-ly, around and around. This pervasively interrelated and ever-changing web of symbols, world view and ethos out of which our lives as persons and peoples is always emerging is what we mean whenever we use the world "culture" in this volume. Let us turn now to an examination of life within the particular symbols, world view and ethos of our contemporary American culture.

Habits of our American Mind and Heart

Deliberate reflection on a culture, particularly one's own and especially one as profoundly diverse and complex as the United States of America's, can seem like an exercise in folly if not grandiosity. We hope to bring a measure of sanity to the task by focusing on a recent analysis of American culture by sociologist Robert Bellah and his associates, Richard Madsen, William Sullivan, Ann Swidler and Steven Tipton. In *Habits of the Heart*, these authors offer a thoughtful and thought-provoking examination of the symbols, world view and ethos of the American culture of the United States, of the individualism and the loneliness which are characteristic of much of our experience.[27] Our summary here will, we hope, whet your appetite for a thorough reading of *Habits of the Heart*.

In an early chapter entitled "Culture and Character: The Historical Conversation," the authors identify four main images of the good life within the history of our version of American culture: the biblical, the republican, the utilitarian and the expressive.[28] These are like four strands which, when woven together, constitute the cultural fabric — the symbols, world view and ethos — of U.S. society. A brief look at each of the strands by way of persons who exemplified them is worthwhile here.

Biblical Individualism

Bellah and his co-authors offer an early Puritan immigrant

leader, John Winthrop, as exemplar of *biblical individualism* in American culture. His vision of life in the new land of America is vividly captured in the following:

> We must delight in each other, make others conditions our own, rejoyce together, mourn together, labor and suf-fer together, always having before our eyes our commu-nity as members of the same body.[29]

In powerful Pauline language and imagery, Winthrop evokes the biblical world view and ethos. This way of life, in its many variations, draws on the stories and imagery of Jewish and Christian scriptures and traditions for its root metaphors of the good life. The ethos and world view of American culture are par-tially constituted by just such a Jewish and Christian, com-munitarian vision of who we are and how we ought to be.

Republican Individualism

The chosen exemplar of the tradition of *republican* (or *civic*) *individualism* in U.S. culture is Thomas Jefferson. Which of us has not absorbed deeply into our world view and way of life Jef-ferson's classical statement of democracy: "All men are created equal"? And while those words must be rewritten in our time in order to include women, the rewriting is by way of expansion and not denial of the authenticity and validity of Jefferson's ideal for our common life. Our republican tradition with its Graeco-Roman roots is utterly unworkable in the absence of citi-zens willing and able to invest in their society as well as their personal interests. The language and imagery of a republic of politically equal persons actively participating in the gover-nance of their society, and the world view and ethos accompany-ing those images are also importantly, albeit only partially, con-stitutive of the culture of the United States.

Utilitarian Individualism

The third strand of our American culture, *utilitarian indi-vidualism*, is exemplified in *Habits of the Heart* in the person of

Benjamin Franklin. The authors note how many of Franklin's "poor Richard" aphorisms — "Early to bed and early to rise, makes a man healthy, wealthy, and wise"; "God helps those who help themselves" — have become ingrained in the world view and ethos of American people.[30] Utilitarian individualism presumes that human beings spend their lives pursuing the individual preferences, needs and interests which they take to be crucial for their existence. The language and imagery, world view and ethos of self-sufficient individuals prospering by virtue of their own industry and initiative is a third partially constitutive strand of what it means to be an American.

Expressive Individualism

The fourth cultural dimension offered by Bellah and his associates, *expressive individualism*, is captured in their description of its exemplar, poet Walt Whitman:

> A life rich in experience, open to all kinds of people, luxuriating in the sensual as well as the intellectual, above all a life of strong feeling, was what he perceived as a successful life.[31]

And again,

> . . . for Whitman, the ultimate use of the American's independence was to cultivate and express the self and explore its vast social and cosmic identities.[32]

The core of expressive individualism as an image of the good life for human beings centers in the notion that each person has a unique core of feeling and intuition that should unfold or be expressed if individuality is to be realized."[33] "Self-actualization" is the popular watchword that names the eschatological vision of expressive individualism.[34] The language of Whitman's lifelong and powerfully liberating song of himself, and the world view and ethos which it evokes, are the fourth partially defining strand of what it means to experience Americanly, to participate in the American cultural community of memory and expectation.

Having traced these formative cultural roots of the United States of America, the authors go on to develop their assessment of the problematics and possibilities of U.S. society in our time. William James observed that the key to understanding an author is catching the center of her or his vision. What is the center of the analysis of contemporary American culture to be found in *Habits of the Heart?* Let's listen:

> Individualism lies at the very core of American culture. There is a biblical and a civic individualism as well as a utilitarian and an expressive individualism. Whatever the differences among the traditions and the consequent differences in their understandings of individualism, there are some things they all share, things that are basic to American identity. We believe in the dignity, indeed the sacredness, of the individual. Anything that would violate our right to think for ourselves, judge for ourselves, make our own decisions, live our lives as we see fit, is not only morally wrong, it is sacrilegious. Our highest and noblest aspirations, not only for ourselves but for those we care about, for our society and for the world, are closely linked to our individualism. We do not argue that Americans should abandon individualism — that would mean to abandon our deepest identity. But individualism has come to mean so many things and to contain such contradictions and paradoxes that even to defend it requires that we analyze it critically, that we consider especially those tendencies that would destroy it from within.[35]

Habits of the Heart is, as its sub-title indicates, an exploration of individualism and commitment in our contemporary American life. It is the conclusion of Bellah and his associates, as of analysts of our culture like David Riesman and Philip Slater before them, that individualism is, for better and for worse, at the core of what it means to be an American.[36]

Bellah and his associates remind us that individualism can be understood and practiced in two quite different ways. First, it can refer to a "belief in the inherent dignity, indeed the sacredness, of the individual."[37] Secondly, it can refer to "a belief that the individual has a primary reality whereas society is a second-order, derived or artificial construct."[38] This crucial distinction lies at the center of the authors' diagnosis of the problems and possibilities of our culture. Let's pursue it a bit further.

Habits of the Heart is not a simple polemic against individualism. To quote the authors once more: "We do not argue that Americans should abandon individualism — that would mean for us to abandon our deepest identity."[39] The first definition of individualism cited above — "a belief in the inherent dignity and, indeed, sacredness of the human person" — is an ideal which has been broadly endorsed by human beings of many cultures over millennia and is clearly held as sacred by Bellah and his co-workers. The polemic in *Habits of the Heart* lies elsewhere.

The basic argument of the authors is with the second definition of individualism cited above — "a belief that the individual has a primary reality whereas society is a second-order, derived or artificial construct." This view of individualism offers the following understanding of human life in the world. In the beginning there were separate individuals with their personal interests to pursue. Society came into being as a complex structure of agreements or contracts among individuals pursuing their interests. Our social world is established voluntarily by individuals who need such an arrangement in order to maximize self-interest more effectively. We first exist as individuals and then form relationships. Society is, in other words, a second-order phenomenon deriving its reality from the choices of individuals; it is a complex instrument existing for the pursuit of individual and group goals. Individually existing persons are the bedrock of human history.

Bellah and his co-authors help us to see that one great danger facing our culture is not individualism *per se*, but the kind of individualism that tears itself loose from the society and culture which is, whether we recognize it or not, its sustaining web. There are other versions of what being an individual means, and the Christian story narrates one of them. Such versions of being a person recognize the intricate ecology of personhood which an "ontological individualism" threatens to destroy. In the words of the authors:

> The question is whether an individualism in which the self has become the main form of reality can really be sustained. What is at issue is not whether self-contained individuals might withdraw from the public sphere to pursue private ends, but whether such individuals are capable of sustaining either a public *or* a private life. If this is the danger, perhaps only the civic and biblical forms of individualism — forms that see the individual in relation to a larger whole, a community and a tradition — are capable of sustaining genuine individuality and nurturing both private and public life.[40]

The four strands just described have been and are now being woven together by U.S. citizens over time into a language, world view and ethos which serve as our collective existential gyroscope. Our collective American memories and expectations bear the indelible marks of biblical, republican, utilitarian and expressive individualism. Together they constitute our principal heritage of models of and for being human. The biblical and republican traditions are particularly valued by Bellah and his associates at this moment of our cultural development, partially because of the keen awareness within these traditions of the fact that human beings do not first exist as individuals and then form relationships of self-interest with others. They counterbalance the unbridled utilitarian and expressive individualism threatening the integrity of the social web which sustains all individuals. Let's develop this point a bit further.

Our individual and collective identities and interests do not exist prior to our relationships, but rather arise out of them. We are continually emerging from a dense web of relationships. To be human is continually to live out of the language, world view and ethos of a culture with a particular history which gives rise to particular possibilities. Relationships with others are so much more than voluntary contracts agreed upon by persons pursuing their individual agendas. This is not to say that such relationships do not exist or that they are bad, but rather to recognize that there is much more to our being-related than the social-contract image can hold.

The central argument of *Habits of the Heart* is that the language of individualism in both its utilitarianism and expressive forms has gradually but decisively become the "native tongue" or (in the authors' usage) the "primary language" of American people in our time. And as we have seen already in our discussion of culture, there is no more profound shaper of a people's world view and ethos, their memories and expectations, than their native language.

But what of the biblical and republican strands which we described as partially constitutive of our American way of life? Bellah and his associates conclude that these languages (which were once the primary definers of our culture) and the world view and ethos associated with them operate as "second languages" in the lives of many U.S. citizens in our time.[41] That is, they are a part of how we speak and think and act, but now a peripheral part when compared with utilitarian and expressive individualism. To be someone's second language is not to be unimportant in affecting their world view and ethos, but only to be less important than their native or primary language. Our first language gives primary form to the everyday world we inhabit and to our style of life within that world. And the first language of Americans in our time, for better and for worse, is that of the utilitarian and the expressive — in its most severely disconnected form, the ontological — individual.

A sustained movement of intentional Christian communities in the United States has an important role to play in our current cultural situation. If we are to have the opportunity as individuals to live deeply out of the more communitarian biblical and re-publican world view and ethos, there must be places where the languages of those traditions loom large in our experience, places where those languages — and the world view and ethos which go with them — are being retrieved in a more primary form. Within American house churches, the utilitarian and ex-pressive forms of individualism which are inevitably part (and within limits, a graceful part) of our way of being American can be challenged and brought into balance by way of an ongoing en-counter with the dangerous communitarian memories and hopes of the biblical tradition.

We hope it is clear that the issue here is *not* negating our-selves as individuals but rather helping ourselves to stay at-tuned to and live in a way that is respectful of the web of our connections to other persons who are also entitled to dignity and respect, as well as to our planet which sustains all human life. It is not that we need to become less as selves, but that our cur-rently dominant forms of selfhood in the United States cry out for integration within a larger sustaining context. Our stories of the individual hero badly need to be in authentic and sustained conversation with stories of the communitarian individual of our biblical tradition and the civic individual of our republican tradition. As we will see in chapter five, one form of such a con-versation is what we call an intentional Christian community.

It is important to observe that the disconnected hyper-indi-vidualism of which *Habits of the Heart* offers a sustained critique appears historically to be much more a male way of shaping existence than a female one. To the extent that Western societies have been patriarchal in character, it should not sur-prise us that male models of and for personhood have pervaded our culture.[42] One of the chief gifts of the contemporary women's movement to American culture is a far more relational, less in-dividualistic vision of what being a person means.[43]

Intentional Christian communities in America are places where the fundamental equality of women and men can be symbolically embodied in inclusive, mutual language in everyday conversation as well as in ritual. Whether in personal relationships or ritual expression, inclusive language is never a cosmetic matter. The testimony of women's stories and of contemporary hermeneutical theory makes it utterly plain that when we systematically exclude a group of persons from our shared vocabulary (as in the common usage in English-speaking cultures of the term "mankind" to refer to all human beings or "he" as a "generic" pronoun) we leave them out of the world. Such language continually reminds everyone who speaks it that women are out of the picture; it systematically disconfirms the existence of women among us.[44] And it is not just this or that instance of being left out of the world that is devastating, but a lifetime's experience of being linguistically excluded, as for example, always hearing and reading of human beings referred to as "mankind."

Given a chance, inclusive ways of telling our stories spawn a more inclusive world view and ethos. To commit ourselves to inclusive language practices is to commit ourselves to inclusive living. To the extent that an intentional Christian community fails to become, in the words of Elisabeth Schüssler Fiorenza, "a dialogical community of equals," it fails to become a Christian community.[45] It fails to become one body. It fails to mediate with fidelity the dangerously liberating memories of the Christian story. Its eucharistic praxis is systematically distorted and distorting.

We have seen that language is never "just words." It is a way of being in the world. Being a member of U.S. society means speaking a certain language, and so does being Christian. There are both powerful congruences and contentious contrasts between the two languages and ways of life. On the congruent side, both traditions cherish every human life. On the contentious side, the ontological individual and the relational web compete for devotion.

Free enterprise, for example, is one expression of our American individualism. It tends to give ethical priority to productive justice: every person has an inalienable right to the products of her or his labor and ingenuity. Our biblical heritage, however, places ethical priority upon distributive justice: every person has a fundamental right to whatever portion of the world's good is necessary for a decent life. For Christians, distributive justice makes a prior claim over productive justice; once the demands of distributive justice are met, however, surplus may accrue in accord with productive justice. It is our contention that the Christian ethos demands that we challenge any form of individualism that would tolerate inequitable distribution of the world's goods. Such a challenge is a redemption of an individualism that violates the web of relationships which sustains us, that fragments the body of Christ.

It is not a matter of replacing our American individualism or free enterprise, but of socially reconstructing them. We cannot but feel helpless when we think as individuals of attempting to change the deep story of massive economic, political and cultural structures. If an individual dreams always and only alone, such dreaming tends toward mere fantasy. But when people retrieve memories that allow them a shared dream, their hope of contributing to a better world is reborn. Part of this rebirth is the recognition that our contribution must be *ours*, not simply my separate effort and yours. In sociological terms, we can best do what needs to be done for our world and ourselves when we are part of mediating structures which help to connect our individual concerns with the megastructures of our culture and political economy. Our next task, therefore, is to suggest a working model for the role that intentional Christian communities — the new house churches — might play as mediating structures in the transformation of our American culture.

Additional Resources

Culture

Contemporary cultural anthropology holds a wealth of description and analysis for persons wishing to grasp how culture operates in our lives. Such a perspective is powerfully presented in Clifford Geertz, *The Interpretation of Cultures* and *Local Knowledge* (N.Y.: Basic Books, 1973 and 1983). The essay from the former collection entitled "Religion as a Cultural System," presents an unforgettable picture of how cultures work and of religion as a sub-system within culture. It contains the anthropological definition of religion perhaps most frequently cited by contemporary theologians. These collections also include other remarkably revealing studies of religious and other cultural sub-systems.

American Culture

There is a rich tradition of analysis of the culture of the United States. As we noted in this chapter, Robert N. Bellah, Richard Madsen, William M. Sullivan, Ann Swidler and Steven M. Tipton, have recently produced *Habits of the Heart* (Berkeley: University of California, 1985), a thought-provoking examination of individualism and commitment in our contemporary American culture. It is must reading for current and prospective members of intentional Christian communities in the United States.

The work of Bellah and his associates stands in a line of distinguished earlier studies of our culture such as those of David Riesman, Nathan Glazer and Reuel Denney, *The Lonely Crowd: A Study of the Changing American Character* (Princeton: Princeton University, 1950); and Philip Slater, *The Pursuit of Loneliness: American Culture at the Breaking Point* (Boston: Beacon, 1970).

Interpretation

Contemporary theories of meaning help us to become aware of the pervasively interpretive character of all human experience. A turn toward hermeneutical models across the scholarly disciplines is the most genuinely exciting and potentially integrating intellectual movement in our time.

In Jesus and the Eucharist (N.Y.: Paulist, 1974) Tad Guzie makes use of an account of how symbols function to help readers reflect on historical and contemporary understandings of the connection between Jesus' life and eucharistic table fellowship among members of Christian communities. The book offers a thoroughly non-supernatural and profoundly spiritual image of the authentic meaning of eucharistic ritual.

In "Interpretation of the Bible and Interpretation Theory," in Robert M. Grant, *A Short History of the Interpretation of the Bible* (Philadelphia: Fortress, 1984, second edition), chapter 16, David Tracy offers a clear and readable discussion of contemporary interpretation (or hermeneutical) theory in the tradition of Heidegger, Gadamer, Ricoeur and Habermas. In chapters 17 and 18 of the same volume, Tracy works out the implications of modern hermeneutics for theological interpretation of scripture within the community of faith today. There is no better point of entry to this important contemporary mode of thought than these three chapters.

Inclusive Language

An Inclusive Language Lectionary: Readings for Years A, B and C (Philadelphia: Westminster; 1983, 1984, 1985) will be helpful to intentional Christian communities wishing to have inclusive language in their liturgical scriptural texts. Other worthwhile resources on this theme include Casey Miller and Kate Swift, *Words and Women* (N.Y.: Doubleday, 1977); and Letty M. Russell (ed.), *The Liberating Word* (Philadelphia: Westminster, 1976). Both of these are readable and informative accounts of issues related to the use of inclusive language. They would serve as a fruitful focus for discussion of this issue in small communities.

Letty M. Russell, *Human Liberation in a Feminist Perspective,* (Philadelphia: Westminster, 1974). In chapter three of this constructive and critical work, "Search for a Useable Past," the author helps us to understand that to be left out of language is to be left out of the world which the language names. The importance of inclusive language with respect both to human beings and to the naming of God is discussed.

Notes

1. An illuminating discussion of the function of exemplary characters within a culture is to be found in Alasdair MacIntyre, *After Virtue* (South Bend: Notre Dame, 1981), pp. 26-29. About these cultural models of and for personhood MacIntyre writes: "A character is an object of regard by the members of the culture generally or by some significant segment of them. He [sic] furnishes them with a cultural and moral ideal." (p. 28) MacIntyre's concept of paradigmatic persons is appropriated and brought to bear on contemporary American society by Robert N. Bellah, Richard Madsen, William M. Sullivan, Ann Swidler and Steven M. Tipton, *Habits of the Heart* (Berkeley: University of California, 1985), pp. 39-51. The authors discuss the "independent citizen," the "entrepreneur," the "manager," and the "bureaucrat" as representative characters in American culture.

2. Catherine M. Mengele, "The Value of My American Citizenship," *San Antonio Light,* December 10, 1985.

3. Quotations taken from presentations by psychologist David Campbell of the Center for Creative Leadership, Greensboro, North Carolina. Blandin Foundation, Grand Rapids, Minnesota, 1985.

4. The loneliness and alienation endemic to contemporary American life is taken up from various perspectives in Peter L. Berger and Richard J. Neuhaus, *To Empower People* (Washington, D.C.: American Enterprise Institute, 1977), pp. 2-3; Gerard Egan and Michael A. Cowan, *People in Systems* (Monterey: Brooks/Cole, 1979), pp. 1-3 and chap. 11; Robert A. Nisbet, *The Quest for Community* (N.Y.: Oxford, 1953), chaps. 1 and 3.

5. The concept of the "double bind" was a ground breaking attempt to understand schizophrenia as the outcome of participation in intensely contradictory patterns of familial communication. The classic 1956 article on the subject by Gregory Bateson and his associates, "Toward a Theory of Schizophrenia," is reprinted together with a number of related articles in Milton M. Berger (ed.), *Beyond the Double Bind* (N.Y.: Brunner/Mazel, 1978).

6. The analysis of culture which informs this section, and indeed the whole text, is based on the work of Clifford Geertz. Geertz refers to his approach to culture as "semiotic." In doing so he means to call our attention to the centrality of symbolic meanings in cultural life. This emphasis is reflected in his definition of culture as "an historically transmitted pattern of meanings embodied in symbols, a system of inherited conceptions expressed in symbolic forms by means of which persons communicate, perpetuate and develop their knowledge about and attitudes toward life." (1973, p. 89).

Geertz's masterful evaluation of human cultures is full of both insightful generalizations about culture as such, and immense respect for the irreducible particularity and diversity of human cultures. Cf. *The Interpretation of Cultures* (N.Y.: Basic Books, 1973), especially chaps. 1-5; and *Local Knowledge* (N.Y.: Basic Books, 1983).

7. On the workings of symbols, cf. Geertz, 1973, pp. 91-94. Geertz's conception of symbol is heavily indebted to Susanne K. Langer, *Philosophy in a New Key* (Cambridge: Harvard, 1957), chaps. 2-5.

Langer's understanding of symbol, and that of the authors of this text, owes a large debt to the analysis of symbolic perception as a mode of experience in the process/relational metaphysics of Alfred North Whitehead. Cf. his *Symbolism: Its Meaning and Effect* (New York: Macmillan, 1927).

8. Human beings do not first perceive bare objects and then label them. We perceive everything as this or that, by relating it to the stock of knowledge which we have acquired through previous experience. Cf. Martin Heidegger, *Being and Time* (N.Y.: Harper and Row, 1962. Translated by John Macquarrie and Edward Robinson), pp. 188-195. For explanations of this crucial but very difficult passage from Heidegger, cf. John Macquarrie, *Martin Heidegger* (Richmond: John Knox Press, 1968), pp. 19-27; and Michael Gelven, *A Commentary on Heidegger's "Being and Time"* (N.Y.: Harper & Row, 1970), pp. 91-101.

That all perception is "perception-as" is a foundational aspect of Martin Heidegger's phenomenological analysis of human existence. It is principally from Heidegger's analysis of how interpretation derives from the basic existential structure of understanding as projection that our contemporary awareness of the inescapability of the "hermeneutical circle" has arisen. Cf. notes 10, 25 and 26 below.

9. Cited in Richard Bandler and John Grinder, *The Structure of Magic* (Palo Alto: Science and Behavior Books, 1975, Volume One), pp. 10-11. Our pervasive linguistic filtering of perception is also examined in Harry Hoijer, "The Sapir-Whorf Hypothesis," in Larry A. Samovar and Richard E. Porter, *Intercultural Communication* (Belmont: Wadsworth, 1972, second edition), pp. 150-158.

10. Perhaps the central assertion of contemporary hermeneutical theory is of the "linguisticality" of all human perception and understanding. As speakers of a language, we are always already participants in an ongoing conversation (i.e., a tradition). In Gadamer's words, language is "the medium of hermeneutical experience." Human interpreting never takes place in a manner uninfluenced by the native language of the ones experiencing. Cf. Hans-Georg Gadamer, *Truth and Method* (N.Y.: Crossroad, 1982. Translation edited by Garrett Barden and John Cumming), pp. 345-366.

Cf. note 25 below.

11. The connection between western culture and the Christian religion is richly explored in part II of Bernard E. Meland, *Faith and Culture* (Carbondale: Southern Illinois University, 1953), and Northrop Frye, *The Great Code* (N.Y.: Harcourt Brace Jovanovich, 1983).

12. On world view, cf. Geertz, 1973, pp. 98-108.

13. An account of such world views is to be found in Mircea Eliade, *Cosmos and History* (N.Y.: Harper & Row, 1954).

14. Cf. Heidegger's phenomenological analysis of what happens when our cultural "equipment" fails to function as it should, 1962, pp. 102-107.

15. On the centrality of symbolic learning vs. genetic programming in human culture, cf. Geertz, 1973, pp. 92-94; and Karl Marx, *Capital* (N.Y.: International Publishers, 1967), pp. 177-78.

16. Cf. W.I. Thomas, *The Child in America* (N.Y.: Knopf, 1928), p. 572. Thomas writes: "If men [sic] define situations as real, they are real in their consequences." This is in effect a restatement (and in these days of feminist critique of patriarchial language and culture) quite an ironic one, of the metaphor of the "hermeneutical circle." Cf. note 25 below.

17. On ethos, cf. Geertz, 1973, pp. 94-98 and 119-123.

18. Contemporary narrative theologians have been insistent on the danger of theological reflection divorcing itself from its founding narratives. Cf. Michael Goldberg, *Theology and Narrative* (Nashville: Abingdon, 1981), pp. 34-35.

19. For a discussion of American culture as "graced" and "disgraced," cf. John F. Kavanaugh, *Following Christ in a Consumer Society* (Maryknoll: Orbis, 1981), chapter two.

20. On moods as an aspect of ethos, cf. Geertz, 1973, pp. 97-8.

21. On the character of American culture as "instrumental activism," cf. Talcott Parsons, *Personality and Social Structure* (N.Y.: The Free Press, 1964), pp. 159-161, 195-198 and 237-239.

22. On the effects of ritual on everyday perception and action, cf. Geertz, 1973, pp. 122-23.

23. Geertz, 1973, pp. 89-90.

24. On the capacity of religious symbols and doctrines to legitimate particular societal arrangements, cf. Peter L. Berger, *The Sacred Canopy* (N.Y.: Doubleday, 1967), chapters one and two.

25. As we approach something to be interpreted, we inevitably relate it to a framework of previous understandings constructed out of prior learning and experience. Whenever an event of interpretation occurs, something makes its way into our preunderstandings, modifying them to some degree. Our preunderstandings make possible all interpretation; all interpretation transforms our preunderstandings. This is the "hermeneutical circle."

We always understand a part (of an object, a story, a self, a world) by relating it to some whole. Whenever we grasp a part, our understanding of the whole is transformed. This is the "hermeneutical circle."

The hermeneutical circle is a metaphor for human existence in the world. Human beings live, move and have their being always and only within the hermeneutical circle. We always interpret as members of a cultural, symbolic, linguistic community. There is no place else for us to stand, no other way for us to exist.

Contemporary philosophical hermeneutics in the tradition of Heidegger, Gadamer, Habermas and Ricoeur is an elaboration on the hermeneutical circle as a metaphor for the human condition. A powerful synoptic statement of the hermeneutical stance and its implications for autentic religious understanding and dialogue in a pluralistic age is to be found in David Tracy, *The Analogical Imagination* (N.Y.: Crossroad, 1981), Chapter 3. For an extremely clear and brief pathway into the vision of contemporary philosophical hermeneutics, cf. Robert M. Grant with David Tracy, *A Short History of the Interpretation of the Bible* (Philadelphia: Fortress, 1984, second edition), chap. 16.

Cf. note 26 below.

26. Heidegger (cf. 1962, pp. 182-195; and Macquarrie, 1968, pp. 19-33) taught us that human existence in the world always entails having future possibilities projected in front of us out of the particular histories from which we are emerging. Human possibilities are always historically grounded. When we begin to make explicit the possibilities we are always sensing for the future in the light and shadow of our particular histories (and we have no other framework in which to put them), we are engaging in *the* uniquely human activity. Its name is interpretation. Its metaphor is the hermeneutical circle.

Every community projects future possibilities in the light and shadow of its always already interpreted history — its great story. Americans and Russians do; Iraquis and Iranians do; South African blacks and Afrikaaners do; Israelis and Palestinians do; British Unionists and Irish Nationalists do. Every living tradition is, in this precise Heideggerian sense, a community of memory and expectation.

As we will stress in Chapter Five of this text, intentional Christian communities construct the future in the light and shadow of a conversation between the great story of Christianity *and* those of their own and other cultures. A powerful treatment of the interplay of memory and expectation in Christian tradition is to be found in Johann Baptist Metz, *Faith in History and Society* (N.Y.: Crossroad, 1980), chaps. 5-13.

27. Bellah et al., 1985.

28. Bellah et al., 1985, chap. 2.

29. Bellah et al., 1985, p. 28.

30. Bellah et al., 1985, p. 32.

31. Bellah et al., 1985, p. 34.

32. Bellah et al., 1985, p. 35.

33. Bellah et al., 1985, p. 334.

34. The classic analysis of "self-actualization" is to be found in Abraham H. Maslow, *Toward a Psychology of Being* (N.Y.: Van Nostrand Reinhold, 1968, second edition). Perhaps no other book's contents (whether accurately understood or not!) became more deeply absorbed into the collective psyche or culture of the "'60s Generation." Walt Whitman, Bellah's exemplar of "expressive individualism" in American culture (cf. note above), is aptly understood as an ancestor of the contemporary emphasis on self-actualization in American culture.

35. Bellah et al., 1985, p. 142.

36. Cf. David Riesman, with Nathan Glazer and Reuel Denney, *The Lonely Crowd: A Study of the Changing American Character* (Princeton: Princeton University, 1950); and Philip Slater, *The Pursuit of Loneliness: American Culture at the Breaking Point* (Boston: Beacon, 1970).

37. Bellah et al., 1985, p. 334.

38. Bellah et al., 1985, p. 334.

39. Bellah et al., 1985, p. 142.

40. Bellah et al., 1985, p. 143.

41. Bellah et al., 1985, p. 154.

42. On the history, anatomy and effects of patriarchy, cf. Elisabeth Schüssler Fiorenza, *Bread not Stone* (Boston: Beacon, 1984), pp. xiv-xvii and chap. 4; Gerda Lerner, *The Creation of Patriarchy* (N.Y.: Oxford, 1986); and Rosemary Radford Reuther, "Feminism and Patriarchial Religion," *Journal for the Study of the Old Testament*, 22 (1982), pp. 54-66.

43. In a historically patriarchal culture such as the American one, the women's movement (which is at its strongest in America) is a major resource for the development of a more relational, less individualistic vision of personhood. Such a vision can be glimpsed in Carol Gilligan, *In a Different Voice* (Cambridge: Harvard, 1982), chaps. 1-3 and 6; and Letty M. Russell, *Human Liberation in a Feminist Perspective* (Philadelphia: Westminster, 1974), chap. 5.

44. On the significance of inclusive language, cf. Russell, 1974, chap. 3; and Casey Miller and Kate Swift, *Words and Women* (N.Y.: Doubleday, 1977). The authors owe a debt of gratitude to particular women in our world who have taught us in various communities about what's really at stake in this issue: Cynthia Miller Cowan, Catherine LaGow, Margie Ryan Boatz, Sandy Bot-Miller, Joan Finlay Vincent, Barbara Lund Strandemo, Mary Melia, Linda Hatch and Mary Dutscher.

Once we have fully appreciated the fact that all perception and understanding — all interpretation — is both made possible and limited by the language of those doing the interpreting (cf. note 10 above), we recognize that to leave persons systematically out of language is to leave them systematically out of the world. An authentically hermeneutical stance is always inclusive, appreciative, critical and mutual.

45. Schüssler Fiorenza, 1984, p. xiv.

Chapter 4

INTENTIONAL CHRISTIAN COMMUNITIES: MEDIATING STRUCTURES IN THE WEB OF SYSTEMS

The house church communities which we have described are made up of Christian persons who have deliberately chosen to cast their lots with other Christian people. This deliberate choice makes them intentional communities rather than simply random gatherings. Despite our legendary cultural loneliness, it is not at all easy for American individualists to cast our lots significantly with anyone outside our primary groups. Contemporary divorce rates in our society seem to suggest that our pursuit of individuality bodes ill even for primary-group commitments. Intentional community is not a "natural" for us. In the first part of this chapter, we will examine closely what it means to participate in an intentional community, for that is part of our Christian vocation.

Just as every individual has his or her being within a vast network of systems, so does each small system live and breathe within the context of much larger systems. In the middle section of this chapter, we will look at the web of our social world from a systems perspective.

We have also seen that intentional Christian communities

are agents of social reconstruction. Their memories are dangerous because they spawn hopes that require that present social arrangements be put under prophetic critique. These small communities have the power to call for change because their members can speak with one voice. That voice is amplified still further when intentional communities form into networks. The final part of this chapter will focus on communities and networks of communities as mediating structures in the world of systems.

We begin exploration in this chapter by examining the specific, *intentional* commitments of Christian communities within our American faith and culture.

Christian Communities as Intentional

As we are using it in this book, the word "intentional" means "deliberate" or "consciously chosen." Adopting this word is our way of highlighting the fact that within the relatively affluent contemporary culture of the U.S., large numbers of persons will ordinarily not be drawn into small communities out of necessity, as has been the case in Latin America. The worldwide movement of intentional Christian communities can be authentically appropriated in and for our version of American culture only in a voluntary and democratic fashion. It is a way of life to which persons must be invited. The kind of community life which we are about to describe in detail cannot and should never be forced on anyone. It must be chosen intentionally.

We want to present a working model of intentional Christian community. We call it a "working model" because it is intended as a practical tool for reflection and action in small communities. Let's begin with a definition. An intentional Christian community is a relatively small group of persons committed to ongoing conversation and shared action along four distinguishable but interrelated dimensions:

— They are consistently committed to a high degree of mutuality in the relationships among them.

— They pursue an informed critical awareness of and an active engagement within the cultural, political and economic megasystems of their society.

— They cultivate and sustain a network of lively connections with other persons, communities and movements of similar purpose.

— They attend faithfully to the Christian character of their community's life.

We have just named the four dimensions of intentional Christian community in thoroughly contemporary language. Terms like "mutuality," "megasystem" and "network" are drawn from the vocabulary of the modern social sciences. But such terms can also be translations, attempts to revivify the ideals of our ancient Christian story in everyday contemporary life, to help us name and envision a form of Christian praxis in and for our time.[1]

"Mutuality," for instance, is a way of naming the *koinonia*, the belonging and equality, the solidarity among persons characteristic of authentic Christian existence. As we saw in Chapter One, *koinonia* pertains to relationships *within* particular small communities as well as to relationships *among* various small communities. As we learn to participate in face-to-face relationships of mutuality, we are actually nurturing *koinonia* among us. As we learn to network effectively with others of common purpose, we are extending and deepening the web of *koinonia* — of belonging and equality — which our Christian story holds to be sacred.

"Pursuing an informed critical awareness of and an active engagement within the cultural, political and economic 'megasystems' of our lives" is simply a contemporary way of naming a form of the *diakonia*, the caring service, to which authentic Christian existence calls us. As we shall see in the two following chapters, "private" Christianity is a profound contradiction of our ancient tradition. Our Christian vocation is radically social or relational. When we learn to reflect together critically and theologically and to engage actively with the world around us in the light of such reflection, we are extending our *diakonia* — our caring and serving presence — into the systems of the contemporary world.

Finally, "to attend faithfully to the Christian character of our community's life" is to keep the Christian *kerygma* with its dangerous memories and transformative hopes at the center of our collective consciousness (and unconsciousness!), and to celebrate that memory and hope together in the sacramental moments of Christian *leitourgia*. In communal and intercommunal rituals of word and sacrament, members of intentional Christian communities keep their personal and collective moods and motivations attuned to the challenging and consoling contours of their sacred story.[2] In so doing, they place the everyday acts of their interaction with one another and the world in the ultimate context of the sacred Christian narratives of justice and love.[3]

Therefore, to say that intentional Christian communities are characterized by mutuality, social engagement, networking and Christian remembrance is to say that these small groups are concretely involved together in the genuine praxis of *koinonia, diakonia, kerygma* and *leitourgia*. It is to say that they are truly ecclesial units, truly church. Many human groups are characterized by one or several of these four attributes; an intentional Christian community is the social form that it is because it intends to strive toward the faithful embodiment of all of them simultaneously.

Claim, Promise, Commitment

Pressing and often overwhelming and demoralizing dilemmas face people in our time — issues of peace, economic and social justice and the rights of women and other oppressed groups. And we have seen how the hyper-individualistic form of contemporary U.S. culture makes solidarity with other persons a dilemma. Later in this chapter we will look at the intricate web of systems which characterizes life in advanced industrial societies like our own. In such a troubled and complex world, it touches the deepest longings of many people to envision the possibility of participating in a group where a high quality of belonging is experienced through mutual relationships, where society and history are engaged and not retreated from, where we feel the common presence of other groups with shared values and purposes, and where the centuries-old conversation called Christian tradition is faithfully and ritually celebrated in and for our time.[4]

This is indeed the four-fold claim and promise of intentional Christian community. But it is a claim not in the sense of ownership, but rather in the sense of a piece of earth to be worked painstakingly and with fidelity. And it is a promise not in the sense of a guarantee, but rather in the sense of a possibility which might unfold into concrete actuality. As we shall see in our discussion of mediating structures, the social form we are calling intentional Christian community does indeed hold the potential for deeply creative interaction with other individuals and with the megasystems of our world. But this creativity will emerge in society and history in a sustainable way only if networks of small Christian communities intentionally not only stake their claims but keep their promises in fidelity with the sacred stories of their tradition.

At one level, a commitment to intentional Christian community is a promise to stay engaged over time with a particular group of persons in the four tasks just described. Such a promise gives the community a special right to our time, energy and care. But at the core, commitment makes our *selves* available to specific others in a privileged way. Something of the highly cherished American privacy and individuality which we examined in Chapter Three is always given up in authentic commitment to intentional community. This is in fact one of the major uphill struggles facing a movement of such communities in a country such as the U.S. with its profoundly individualistic and autonomous world view and ethos. On the other hand, the distress many Americans feel in our collective "pursuit of loneliness" is, as we have seen, a powerful cultural incentive to a new form of belonging.

Beyond granting a particular group of persons privileged access to our selves, a commitment to intentional community is an acknowledgment of the fact that being-related is central to human existence. It is a way not merely of coping with, but even of celebrating, life as participation in the web of systems which we are about to explore here. It is, as we will see, a commitment to participation in a particular form of mediating structure within that web.

What we acknowledge in committing ourselves to intentional community is that our individual and collective identities do not exist prior to our relatings, but arise out of them.[5] Our sense of identity—as individuals, Christians, Americans, etc.—emerges from and is continually being transformed within our concrete web of connections to life.

Commitment to the shared life and work of any kind of intentional community is a recognition of the significance and pervasiveness of human life as irreducibly relational. Commitment to the shared life and work of an intentional *Christian* community is an acknowledgement of the religious character of our being-related. Christians in intentional community are allowing the profoundly relational character of their sacred narrative to shape their existence profoundly. At the center of the dangerously liberating memory which is Christian tradition is a communitarian or relational vision of human life in the world. In such a vision my life is never just about me, it is always about us as well. We matter, all of us, living and dead.

We have said that commitment to intentional Christian community entails a promise over time. There are many worthwhile experiences that can happen in an hour or a weekend or a month; intentional community is not one of them. There is an issue of continuity here, of the staying power of our claims and promises. It has been observed that when an intimate relationship is working well there is a strong tendency for persons to commit and re-commit themselves to it. It is as if there is a natural strain toward permanence in creative, intimate relationships.[6]

The promise that is commitment to intentional Christian community is like that. It is generated and regenerated in the everyday acts of community life: in our mutuality, our collective engagement with the world, our standing in common cause with others of similar purpose, and our shared practices of memory and anticipation in word and sacrament; that is to say, in our shared praxis of *koinonia, diakonia, kerygma* and *leitourgia*. In sustaining the four-fold pattern of these everyday acts over time, we come to feel the efficacy of belonging to intentional Christian community flowing into and out of us.

What Intentional Community is Not

The Whiteheads have taught us to recognize that community is not the same kind of social form as a family, that it is both less and more.[7] Intentional community is less than family in the sense that the expectable level of intimacy and mutual inter-dependence required within it is typically not at the level required to sustain creative family life.[8] It is more because intentional communities have commitments which reach beyond their immediate boundaries.

Neither is community the same kind of entity as a formal organization.[9] Such social forms (e.g., corporations and governmental agencies) come into being in order to carry out particular, well-defined activities (e.g., manufacturing and retailing some item profitably or administering a county's welfare budget efficiently). They are ordinarily highly concerned with accomplishing their tasks as efficiently as possible and tend to be less concerned with the needs, values and well-being of their "personnel." Although a modern, enlightened formal organization would never put it this way, there is a very real sense in which its people are "human capital," one more resource required to accomplish its mission. To make this observation is not totally to criticize such social forms, although such an instrumental view of persons does demand a strong critique.[10] Our intent at this point is merely to distinguish among primary groups, formal organizations and communities as social forms with important differences.

Like formal organizations, intentional Christian communities also have important tasks to accomplish; their members do not gather just for the sake of being together. As mediating structures, they have social as well as intracommunal tasks. But unlike formal organizations, the needs, values and well-being of members of intentional community are co-equal in importance with the community's tasks.

The Whiteheads have captured this "like and not like" characteristic of community by referring to it as a "hybrid" or "intermediate" social form. That is, communities have some of the personal, relational orientation associated with primary groups like families, and some of the task orientation of formal organizations like bureaucracies. In Chapter Two, we examined various concrete cultural expressions of this dual focus in small Christian communities emerging around the world.

An intentional Christian community stressing its own internal or private relationships and needs to the exclusion of its task of creative engagement with its world is more primary group than community. A community focusing on its public tasks to the exclusion of a deep concern for mutuality in its relationships is more formal organization than community. To participate in an intentional Christian community is a complex and challenging process largely because it demands of its members high levels of *both* task and relationship orientations if it is to work.

Having taken an initial look at the character of small Christian communities as intentional and as hybrid social forms, we must now turn our attention to the social context within which such communities operate today.

The Context of Intentional Christian Communities: An Ecology of Human Systems

Small Christian communities exist as ecclesial units within a complex arrangement of systems, an ecological web. "Ecology" is the name we give to the study of relationships between organisms and their environment. We are coming to realize that the ecology of all life is systemic in character, that what happens and fails to happen in our world for good and ill is a matter of relationships and their effects on everything and everyone concerned. We have begun to accept the fact that no aspect of life can be adequately understood apart from a profound awareness of its context.[11] Human beings are slowly but surely arriving at an awareness of our natural and social ecological web; we are developing the capacity to live in a systems world.[12] Christian communities can simply not afford to ignore their embeddedness within this web of systems.

Members of Christian communities begin to appreciate the systemic character of our world when we recognize that anyone's "individual" becoming really refers to how she or he is emerging from the particular historical contexts — planetary, genetic, familial, social, economic, political and cultural — of life.[13] The futures which we might create together are, for better and for worse, in continuity with the history of events within the webs of relationship just named. We are always already situated within a particular world with a concrete history; the futures we might create will always bear the mark of our context and its history.[14]

To live responsibly in a systems world is to have one's life profoundly shaped by the awareness that only to a limited extent is existence an individual matter. It is to realize that, like it or not, we are all in this together. To paraphrase Teilhard de Chardin, our past is not part of history possessed by us totally, but rather all of history possessed by us partially.[15] By the same token our future is not an isolated piece of what might be which we own autonomously, as if it were our private property; it is part of the common possible futures of our species within the universe itself.

It is illuminating for members of Christian communities to understand our world as a complex web of interrelated systems. In fact we are convinced that the principal commitments of such communities in our time — peace, the full inclusion of women and other formerly "invisible" people within society, economic and social justice worldwide, and intercultural communication and respect — cannot be adequately understood and addressed apart from a practical systematic analysis of human society and history. In order to foster that kind of understanding for members of Christian communities, we will present a brief overview of the web of systems within which the everyday lives of persons in our culture are played out and then use that overview in order to situate the particular social form called community.

The Web of Human Systems: A Working Model

This model of the systemic web of our lives is organized on two levels: microsystems and megasystems.[16] Like all models it is a simplification. In order to be useful it should be complex enough to capture something of the interrelatedness of the human systems which are the context in which Christian communities must survive and thrive, and simple enough to be useful for reflective action by community members.[17]

The Microsystems Level

These are the small, immediate systems of our everyday lives.[18] Families or other living groups, work teams, support groups, citizen boards and certain voluntary associations organized around causes or interests are all examples of microsystems. In contemporary U.S. society, most of our time is spent interacting in a complex variety of microsystems — families, workplaces, classrooms, church groups, etc. The quality of these relationships obviously has an enormous effect on people's sense of well-being and quality of life.

The structure and dynamics of any microsystem constitute a kind of dance, in which the participants have interlocking, mutually reciprocal roles. The effects of this dance on individual participants are indeed profound; in fact, it is clear that we must carefully rethink what "individual becoming" means in the light of our contemporary understanding of systems. For it is increasingly evident that no person in a system is an island, immune or cut off from the system's effects. Intrapersonal events in microsystems are in important ways a matter of internalizing and otherwise reacting to a system's repeating pattern of relationships.[19]

The extent and lasting effects of our interdependence within important systems is further revealed when we recognize that typical patterns of behavior and feelings are not merely ways that people cope while they are members of a particular system, which can then be easily dropped when and if they leave it. The pattern of events in the lives of adult "graduates" of families attests to the ongoing effects of the systemic roles which we learned to play intitially in order to survive within important systems. Those roles constitute the social and emotional foundations of our individual personalities. They provide our basic training for personhood. A microsystem is not just an external place where autonomous individuals hang around for a while; it is at the center of our web of relationships. And that web is the source of the selves we are becoming.[20]

Remaining at the microsystems level, it is important to be aware of the networks of microsystems in our lives.[21] Thinking this way can help us to remember that we are not just a family member and then later a participant on a work team and still later a participant in a faith-sharing group; rather, we belong to a set of microsystems simultaneously. The pattern of reciprocal effects among our microsystems constitute another part of the overall systems context within which Christian communities arise. What happens in our living group can have profound effects on our participation in our work group and vice versa. Indeed, one of the most common complaints of contemporary Americans is that there is never enough time and energy for satisfying participation in our network of microsystems.

Like individual persons within a microsystem, the individual systems within the network of microsystems affect and are affected by each other. Together they constitute a system of systems, a complex and recurring pattern of mutually influential interaction within which our personal development is always unfolding. Our network of microsystems is like a smaller web within a larger one. This larger web we call the "megasystems."

The Megasystems Level

This term refers first of all to those large institutions and organizations which, while not as immediately present to us in everyday life as our microsystems, have profound effects on our existence.[22] The institutions and organizations of government, the economy, mass media, religion and education, which are one part of the web of megasystems, have profound and continuous effects on events within our microsystems. The smaller and more personal systems can and do also affect megasystems, though we typically and understandably experience the influence as running primarily in the other direction. A bit later in this chapter we will begin to consider how microsystems like intentional Christian communities might affect larger systems; we'll continue that exploration in more depth and specificity in Chapter Six. For now, let's concentrate on the influence of larger systems on smaller ones.

The microsystems of U.S. society, including small Christian communities, are situated today within the larger socioeconomic context called an "advanced industrial society." Such a society is one which has undergone two important transformations in its basic economic structure. The first of these is a shift of the majority of workers from agriculture to various industries. The second, which continues rapidly in American society today, is the movement of a significant number of workers from industrial to service occupations. Thus, an advanced industrial society is one in which a large proportion of the labor force is employed in retailing, health, education, government, etc.[23] Such a society requires an incredibly intricate network of production and distribution, transportation, communication, government and legal systems.[24] This interlocking network of large, influential institutions and organizations is one aspect of megasystems.

Advanced industrial societies did not appear in the world full blown; they evolved over the course of human history. During the evolution of megasystems, the economic role of microsystems, like the family, has undergone a significant transformation. Let's take a moment to look at an example of such a transformation, one which by analogy will speak to us about the importance of megasystem events for the life of small Christian communities.

Until quite recently the economic division of labor in advanced industrial society (a megasystem reality) had tended to send males out into the world outside the home to provide the material resources necessary for their family's survival. It had likewise tended to keep females at work inside the home, providing the social and emotional resources required by their families. Most men and women in such a society didn't experience a clear moment of personal choice about whether to go out into the economic marketplace or work at home; it was a matter of fitting into the economic realities, the megasystem rules, of their time. And those rules had (and still have) major effects on all persons and all levels of systems.

These megasystem rules fostered the economic dependency of women, who were expected to take up their economic roles within the home. This meant that many of the educational and on-the-job experiences which allowed men to pursue economic security outside the home were systematically denied to women. When a woman has been outside the employment mainstream for a significant period of time, it is difficult if not impossible for her to move outside the home and make a living adequate to support a family. For similar reasons, she probably has no version of the pension plan or other forms of economic security which her husband has been steadily accruing over the years by virtue of his employment outside the home. As a consequence, she typically faces bleak economic prospects on her own.

Sometimes the very bleakness of these prospects kept (and keep) women in marital relationships where they are victims of various kinds of abuse. We now know clearly that marital relationships characterized by such desperate dependency and abuse predispose all family members to dependent and abusive patterns of relationship, not just during their childhoods but in their adult lives as well.[25] Clearly such an economic situation is in no sense a result of the personal decisions of individuals; it is a megasystemic reality with complex social and historical causes. This example illustrates the power of large systems over the course of individual lives and the functioning of microsystems.

The megasystem exerts powerful formative effects on the functioning of all other levels of systems and, therefore, on the development of all persons. Its functioning is likewise affected by them. The megasystem does not unilaterally determine events elsewhere within the web of life, but its effects are felt always and everywhere. Small Christian communities are of course not exempt from these effects.

The other dimension of the megasystem refers not to particular persons, organizations or institutions, but rather to the culture that is always forming and being formed by them.[26] Culture itself affects and is affected by the ways that the other levels of systems take shape.

As we saw in Chapter Three, culture is an inherited set of understandings and practices which organize a people's life. It is a world of shared meanings, which is carried and transmitted in symbols, especially language. As persons become acculturated, which always happens within the web of systems just described, they learn to experience and to understand their worlds in specific ways. They come to take for granted a particular assumptive world or map of reality.

Culture lends its shape to and is shaped by the structure and dynamics of microsystems as well as those of the large institutions and organizations just described. The pattern of events within the whole systemic web of our lives emerges from complex, multi-directional interactions between microsystems and megasystems. No level dictates events at lower or higher levels, but only influences them, albeit sometimes so profoundly as to appear almost as a determining force. Intentional Christian communities will certainly be affected by events in the web of systems in which they live, and *may* affect those events as well.

We saw in Chapter Three that individualism and instrumental activism seem to be two of the core elements — the central meanings — in the deep story of what it means to live the U.S. form of American life.[27] These cultural givens rinse through and affect all levels of systems in our collective life, including those microsystems called intentional Christian communities. But intentional Christian communities as we understand them are not only microsystems, but also mediating structures.

Intentional Christian Communities as Mediating Structures

As we have seen, the life of persons and peoples is a complex pattern of systemic interactions. While by no means always symmetrical or equal in their effects, these interactions are always reciprocal: all persons and systems are affected for better and for worse by their participation within the systemic web and have their effects on that web. We live within a world of systems, of mutual influence. No vital, sustainable movement of Christian communities is possible within the American context unless its relationship to the web of human systems at both micro-

and mega-levels is carefully taken into account. Even then it won't be easy!

Intentional Christian communities are free, indeed required in many instances, to challenge how events are taking shape within the web of systems which constitutes their society. Sometimes that is the very reason for their coming into existence. And such communities are always interacting within the web of systems, being affected by as well as affecting its character. If such communities have not fallen prey to the Robinson Crusoe fallacy, then they recognize that there is literally no place outside the web of systems where they can live, move and have their being. Chapter Six of this book explores how intentional communities can engage creatively and prophetically with the larger systems which shape our lives so profoundly.

What is the unique character of an intentional Christian community within this complex dance of systems?

Persons in our society routinely move back and forth between smaller and more personal microsystems and the larger and impersonal megasystems.[28] Because these larger systems are so often alienating and depersonalizing in their effects, the citizens of complex advanced industrial societies often feel no choice but to seek personal meaning and belonging within the smaller, face-to-face systems. Because we so often feel relatively helpless about such things as inflation, consumerism, and foreign policy, we understandably tend to leave them to others and turn to family, friendship groups and community for acknowledgement and feelings of efficacy.

But there is a two-fold problem with this common and understandable strategy for coping with the events of life in the contemporary world. First, it tends to alienate us further from the larger systems which have and will continue to have so much effect on possibilities for life in our country and on our planet. As a consequence our political and economic order — the bedrock of any society — can lose legitimacy in the hearts and minds of more and more of its participants. And we can be tempted to abdicate our proper roles as *bona fide* participants in the institutions of government, economy, church and culture — to leave the guidance of all of that in "their" hands. In our absence these megasystems go right on having massively important effects on everyone's lives. So genuinely democratic public order among us becomes more and more difficult to sustain.[29]

Second, the capacity of microsystems to carry the entire weight of meaning and involvement for us is actually quite limited. How can families and communities possibly counterbalance the massive alienating effects of society and culture on the large scale? Clearly, they cannot do so alone. Culture, politics and the economy have major effects on what is likely to occur at the level of microsystems. Events within the micro-level of systems are so often at the mercy of events in the mega-level that it often seems that at best the smaller and more personal systems of our lives can offer us a kind of "haven in a heartless world." The increasing fragility and vulnerability of these havens is more and more apparent.

Vital intentional Christian communities are always more than islands of belonging and support for their members. They can in fact operate as one potential counterweight to the retreat from larger systems into smaller ones. This is so because of their capacity to function as mediating structures.[30] Mediating structures have both internal and external dimensions. They are a place where persons are known personally and related to mutually (the internal dimension), *and* where they can address the larger political, economic and cultural forces of their age in solidarity with others (the external dimension). Intentional Christian communities, like neighborhood councils, professional support groups and other forms of voluntary association, can function as transformative mediating structures within the web of systems. Such communities mediate the dangerous memories and transformative hopes of the Christian tradition in and for the social structures and cultural patterns of their time and place.

An intentional community, then, is not an enclave within the systems world or an island isolated from its effects. As a mediating structure it is a full participant in the world of human and natural systems. It is a particular form of system in which we can participate. One of its defining characteristics is precisely that it is neither strictly internal nor merely external but deliberately takes a stance of mediation between these two crucially important sectors — the micro and the mega — within the web of our lives. An intentional *Christian* community takes its mediating stance in the spirit of justice and love. The social form called intentional Christian community is thus one potentially very important response to the critical systemic issues of our time. We will explore the internal side of participation in intentional Christian community in Chapter Five of this book, and the external side in Chapter Six.

Additional Resources

Community

In *Community of Faith* (N.Y.: Seabury, 1982), Evelyn Eaton and James D. Whitehead aim at clarifying the nature and possibilities of participation in communities of faith in a pluralistic age. The questions for reflection and discussion accompanying each chapter make the text a particularly useful working tool for small communities. Of special interest are chapters 2-6 on "Clarifying the Meaning of Community," and chapters 8-11 on "Participating in Community."

In "Households of Faith in the Coming Church," *Worship,* 57/3 (1983), pp. 237-255, David N. Power draws on sociology, theology and liturgical studies in a masterful historical analysis of the current emergence of small groups of Christians banding together in small, non-traditional ecclesial structures. Particularly enlightening are the parallels he develops between our time and the twelfth and thirteenth centuries. Because Power understands the emergence of households of faith for the coming church precisely as a contemporary movement of ecclesial renewal with important historical precedents, this essay reminds us that small house church communities in our time need not be understood as anti-church. A careful shared reading and discussion of this essay will enrich, inspire and lend valuable historical perspective to the members of any intentional Christian community.

Systems

In *People in Systems* (Monterey: Brooks/Cole, 1979), Gerard Egan and Michael A. Cowan present a model for those who are interested in human development *and* in the structure of the various levels of human systems that provide the sociocultural context or environment of that development. A companion volume entitled *People in Systems: Personal and Professional Applications* (Monterey: Brooks/Cole, 1979) by Michael A. Cowan, Gerard Egan and Norman Hetland presents practical exercises coordinated with the chapters of *People in Systems.* The exercises are aimed at promoting systematic reflection on one's own developmental issues and systems context, as well as enabling others to do so.

The systems metaphor looms large in our contemporary world view. Ervin Laszlo offers a brief and very readable introduction to this perspective in *The Systems View of the World* (N.Y.: Braziller, 1972). The text introduces readers to a systems way of thinking about the physical and social worlds.

In *Organizations in Modern Life* (San Francisco: Jossey-Bass, 1977), Herman Turk analyzes contemporary society as an aggregate of large scale organizations. He illuminates the patterns of interdependence among large scale social networks, and shows the processes that link up the massive bureaucratic substructure of advanced industrial societies.

Mediating Structures

The concept of mediating structures is developed by Peter Berger and Richard J. Neuhaus in *To Empower People* (Washington, D.C.: American Enterprise Institute, 1977). The authors define mediating structures precisely as social forms which provide a link between the small primary systems and the large mega-structures of modern life. They explore the potential of neighborhoods, families, churches and voluntary associations to play mediating roles in our lives.

Notes

1. That translation is an apt metaphor for interpretation, and in many ways its exemplar, has been suggested by Hans-Georg Gadamer in his master work, *Truth and Method* (N.Y.: Crossroad, 1982. Translation edited by Garrett Barden and John Cumming), pp. 345-351.

2. An illuminating exposition of the effects of ritual on the moods and motivations of participants is to be found in Clifford Geertz, "Religion as a Cultural System" in *The Interpretation of Cultures* (N.Y.: Basic Books, (1973), pp. 94-98, 112-114 and 119-123.

A reflection on contemporary American culture from the perspective of Geertz's analysis of religious symbol and ritual can be found in Michael A. Cowan, "Sacramental Moments" in Regis Duffy (ed.) *Alternative Futures of Worship*, Volume I (Collegeville: Liturgical Press, 1987), pp. 29-55.

3. In "Ethos, World View, and the Analysis of Sacred Symbols" Geertz analyzes the ways in which religious symbols related the ethos and world view of a people to an ultimate or sacred context. Cf. Geertz, 1973, pp. 126-141.

4. The unavoidable role of tradition understood as the ongoing interpretation or conversation among persons concretely located in particular linguistic histories is developed in Gadamer, 1982, pp. 245-253.

5. The internally creative role of relationships in the ongoing emergence of human identities is a core dimension of the process/relational metaphysics of Alfred North Whitehead. Cf. his *Process and Reality* (N.Y.: Macmillan, 1978, corrected edition edited by David Ray Griffin and Donald W. Sherburne).

The implications of Whiteheadian metaphysics for our understanding of human identity and relationships are developed in Michael A. Cowan, "Emerging in Love," in Paul W. Pruyser (ed.), *Changing Views of the Human Condition* (Macon: Mercer, 1987).

Our understanding of human interrelatedness in this text is also profoundly indebted to Martin Heidegger. Cf. his *Being and Time* (N.Y.: Harper & Row, 1962. Translated by John Macquarrie and Edward Robinson), pp. 149-168. Cf. also John Macquarrie, *Martin Heidegger* (Richmond: John Knox, 1968), pp. 17-19.

6. Cf. Andrew M.Greeley, *The New Agenda* (Garden City: Doubleday, 1973), p.143.

7. Cf. Evelyn Eaton and James D. Whitehead, *Community of Faith* (N.Y.: Seabury, 1982), pp. 25-27.

8. Whitehead and Whitehead, 1982, p. 27 and chap. 3.

9. Whitehead and Whitehead, 1982, p. 28 and chap. 3.

10. On the possibilities of human systems as contexts for genuine mutuality, cf. Gerard Egan and Michael A. Cowan, *People in Systems* (Monterey: 1979), chap. 11.

11. Gregory Bateson was a major modern prophet regarding the centrality of context in our understanding of anything, and of meaning as the context for

our understanding of events in the human world. For a sample of his powerful and disturbing way of thinking contextually cf. "Form, Substance, and Difference" in his *Steps to an Ecology of Mind* (N.Y.: Ballantine, 1972), especially pp. 458-460, and his *Mind and Nature: A Necessary Unity* (N.Y.: Dutton, 1979).

12. A readable introduction to systems thinking can be found in Ervin Laszlo, *The Systems View of the World* (N.Y.: Braziller, 1972). For a systems model aimed at illuminating the tasks of the human-service professions, including counseling, education and ministry, cf. Egan and Cowan, 1979.

13. Cf. Cowan, 1987, section three.

14. The understanding of human life in the world as an ongoing projection of possible futures in the light and shadow of actual histories — of human existence as "thrown projection," as irreducibly historical or temporal — derives from the hermeneutical phenomenology of Martin Heidegger. Cf. Heidegger, 1962, Division Two: "Dasein and Temporality."

For an excellent brief "translation" (as interpretation) of Heidegger's temporal or historical analysis of human existence, cf. Macquarrie, 1968, pp. 19-41.

David Tracy appropriates Heidegger's metaphor of "thrown projection" to illuminate the inevitably historical stance of human interpreters in *The Analogical Imagination* (N.Y.: Crossroad, 1981), where he writes: "The fact is that an insistence upon the hermeneutical understanding of philosophy and theology is not a search for that 'middle ground' beloved by 'moderates' but an articulation of the only ground upon which any one of us stand: the ground of real finitude and radical historicity in all hermeneutical understanding." (p.103)

The fundamental way in which we move out of our concrete pasts and toward particular possibilities is *interpretation*. It is precisely in that sense that human existence itself can be described as hermeneutical.

15. this sentence is a paraphrase of Teilhard de Chardin who wrote: "*My* matter is not a *part* of the universe that I possess *totaliter*: it is the *totality* of the universe possessed by me *partialiter*." Cf. *Science and Christ* (N.Y.: Harper & Row, 1968), pp. 12-13.

16. The model of levels of systems presented here is derived from Egan and Cowan, 1979. Cf. pp. 70-72 for an overview.

17. On the two criteria for useful models, cf. Egan and Cowan, 1979, p. 6.

18. Egan and Cowan, 1979, pp. 72-79. Note that "microsystems" are also called "personal settings" in the 1979 text.

19. On microsystem interaction as co-creative dance, cf. Cowan, in press, section three, and Virginia Satir, *Peoplemaking* (Palo Alto: Science and Behavior Books, 1972), chaps. 4-8.

20. We now recognize that socialization in human systems of all kinds is a life-long phenomenon. For a classic statement cf. Orville G. Brim and Stanton Wheeler, *Socialization after Childhood* (N.Y.: Wiley, 1966). This ongoing socialization is profoundly relational. Brim writes, for example, that ". . . most of what is learned from socialization in childhood, and indeed throughout life, is a series of complex interpersonal relationships." (p. 8)

21. Egan and Cowan, 1979, chap. five.

22. Egan and Cowan, 1979, chap. six.

23. For an introduction to the anatomy and evolution of large scale socioeconomic structures in the contemporary world, cf. Gerhard and Jean Lenski, *Human Societies* (N.Y.:McGraw-Hill, 1982, fourth edition).

24. A classic treatment of the role of large scale, interlocking organizations and institutions in contemporary advanced industrial societies can be found in Herman Turk, *Organizations in Modern Life* (San Francisco: Jossey-Bass, 1977).

25. The pervasive, profound and long lasting effects of growing up in a particular kind of dysfunctional microsystem — the "alcoholic family" — have been well-documented in Sharon Wegscheider, *Another Chance* (Palo Alto: Science and Behavior Books, 1981), chaps. 6-10. Another widely read text on this subject is Janet Geringer Woititiz's *Adult Children of Alocoholics* (Hollywood, FL: Health Communications, 1983).

26. Egan and Cowan, 1979, chap. 7.

27. On culture understood as story with deep structures and variegated surface expressions, cf. Claude Levi-Strauss, *Myth and Meaning* (N.Y.: Schocken, 1979), and Stephen Crites, "The Narrative Quality of Experience," *Journal of the American Academy of Religion,* 39 (1971), pp. 295-311. Note that in the Crites essay "deep" and "surface" are rendered as "sacred" and "mundane."

28. The movement of contemporary persons between micro- and megastructures is well and briefly described by Peter Berger and Richard John Neuhaus in *To Empower People* (Washington, D.C.: American Enterprise Institute), pp. 1-8.

29. In order to sustain a genuinely democratic public order, a people must be able voluntarily to regulate the direction of their collective life in the service of a consensus about values. In the classical tradition of American social thought, a society's capacity for this sort of regulation is referred to as "social control." It is important to stress that, contrary to the connotations of most contemporary persons, social control as used in this tradition refers to a *voluntary*, i.e., non-coercive, collective activity.

The historical sociological understanding of how members of a democratic society act together voluntarily in the service of shared values is presented in Morris Janowitz, "Sociological Theory and Social Control," *American Journal of Sociology,* (81/1), 1975, pp. 82-108. The concept of social control is employed by Janowitz to examine the integrity and stability of the American political economy in *Social Control of the Welfare State* (Chicago: University of Chicago, 1976), and in *The Last Half-Century* (Chicago: University of Chicago, 1978). Janowitz's is a thought-provoking macro-social analysis, thoroughly grounded in available empirical data on American society in the twentieth century.

30. Berger and Neuhaus, 1977, p. 2. The authors proceed to examine the potential of neighborhoods, families, churches and voluntary associations as mediating structures.

Chapter 5

MEMBERS OF ONE ANOTHER: MUTUALITY IN THE INTENTIONAL CHRISTIAN COMMUNITY

Intentional Community as a Double-Edged, Public Conversation

We have seen a movement at work in the world, reshaping the structures of church for many Christians. This new emphasis upon community and upon lay responsibility for its nurture and destiny is both a retrieval and something new. It is a retrieval because the house church was a regular form of Christian togetherness until the middle of the fourth century. But it is a new thing too, because the contemporary cultures in which it is now arising face different problems and ask different questions of their world and their churches.

As we surveyed the many different forms of intentional Christian communities springing up across the earth, we noted their great variety. That is to be expected, because human cultures are far from uniform and the interaction between anyone's faith and culture is an intimate one.[1] Modern anthropology has taught us that human cultures are in fact dizzyingly diverse.[2] We have likewise discovered that there are no cultures without sacred symbols, symbols which allow their members to locate their everyday lives within an ultimate context of meaning.[3]

In Chapter Three we examined the workings of U.S. culture, searching for aspects of it which militate against a strong and viable movement of intentional Christian communities here, as well as aspects which may nurture such a movement. Then we looked at intentional communities as mediating structures within our culture, and at how such communities have the capacity to join hands by networking. This chapter and the next are about ways in which intentional Christian communities in American culture can take seriously the symbiosis that always connects our faith and our culture. In order to illuminate that intimate connection, we want to begin by drawing an analogy between the life of an intentional community and an important contemporary understanding of how theology ought to be done. For too long, theology has seemed to most of us like an esoteric discipline far removed from Christians' daily concerns. But theology, like church itself, is being returned to the People of God, a phenomenon which Thomas Clarke has in mind when he observes that "the primary *situation* of theological reflection as an historical phenomenon is neither the seminary nor the university but the basic Christian community."[4]

We begin with a simple statement. Then we must complicate it a bit, and soon return to the simple form. A Christian community embraces the Christian "fact": something did happen once upon a time that has continued throughout nearly 20 centuries to make history in the world, even as it reconstitutes itself over and over and over. A Christian community also embraces the cultural "facts" of its immediate situation. It is committed to caring for its present earthly, historical "fact." When a community tries to correlate the Christian "fact" with its present "fact," it usually notices that there are some identical elements in both, some merely similar elements in both, and some deeply contrasting or even hostile elements between them.

Our history shows us that sometimes the Christian "fact" levels a prophetic and corrective critique upon the cultural "fact." In our time and culture, the pastoral letters of the U.S. bishops on peace and economic justice exemplify such a critique.[5] And sometimes the cultural "fact" levels a similarly prophetic and corrective critique upon the Christian "fact." In our time and culture, the feminist critique of patriarchal abuses of power in Western history and society has contributed mightily to an impassioned critique of those same patriarchial structures within the Christian churches.[6] What all this tells us is that cultural and Christian "facts" are always in some form of mutually appreciative and critical tension and interaction with each other.[7] David Tracy's work illuminates the character of formal theological reflection precisely as an ongoing mutually critical conversation between interpretations of the Christian "fact" and interpretations of the cultural "fact."[8]

Like theology, an intentional Christian community involves a vivid conversation between faith and culture. Notice that in Chapter Four we have already explored this kind of interaction between community and culture from one perspective in our discussion of intentional communities as mediating structures. A faith community is never "over here" while its culture remains "over there." There is no "us and culture." There is only "us-in-culture" and "culture-in-us."

A particular form of conversation always occurs within an authentic community; this is the *primary* or family-like side of community life. There is also the conversation which always occurs between the community and its world; this is what we have called the *secondary* or organizational dimension of an intentional community's life. In both its internal and external forms, the conversation called intentional community will have mutually appreciative and critical dimensions, that is to say, such conversation always involves both compassionate understanding and constructively critical challenge between Christian and contemporary "facts." An intentional Christian community is not just a place where this always-two-dimensional kind of conversation occurs; it is precisely such conversation that constitutes such a community.

Now we must take on some complexities. In the text just above, the word "fact" always appears in quotation marks. This is to call your attention to the increasingly widespread recognition that there is no such thing as an uninterpreted "fact."[9] As we noted in Chapter Three, there is no more powerful influence on our assumptive worlds of meaning than our native language. Our very selves in fact are radically constituted by culture as well as by personal and societal history.[10] The lives of persons and peoples are far more like perpetually unfinished narratives than like oak-tree-from-acorn, automatically unfolding essences. If they are to remain alive, narratives require retelling and reinterpretation from age to age.

Often in order to hear what another person's words mean, I must remind myself that whatever we may have in common, he or she has long interpreted many things differently than I. If this is so, then all of that accumulated history cannot fail to affect our understandings of the present "fact." Creative conversation requires that we attempt to grasp others' meanings in a way that is faithful to their perspective, while recognizing that we have no other vantage point than our own from which to interpret them. And it is very, very hard work for two persons or two communities consistently to connect horizons in mutually respectful conversation.[11]

Now to a second complexity. How we interpret any "fact" determines what that "fact's" impact upon us will be. When we say what a "fact" means to us, we are always saying something about how it enters into our understanding of how life itself goes. In other words, our meanings give shape to our possibilities as persons and peoples. "Facts" have consequences; they make a difference. The most important "facts" are those that make the most difference in what futures it is possible for us to project. A "fact's" meaning is that "fact's" consequences for how we shall be in the world. Whenever we interpret "the facts," and we do so constantly, we are participating in the ongoing creation of the world we must inhabit.[12] And being-in-the-world is always a public issue. We are always affecting and being affected by others' interpretations of "the facts."

An intentional Christian community recognizes that its conversation is its ongoing interpretation of the Christian "fact" and the cultural "facts" of its time and place.[13] It is intent upon the public meanings and consequences of that conversation, upon the difference it makes for our lives in the contemporary world — for the futures we want to build and those we want to repudiate. Mutual, inclusive, appreciative and critical conversation-as-interpretation is not merely one thing an intentional community does; such conversation constitutes the warp and woof of authentic intentional community.

Back to simplicity. In whatever language their "facts" are named, human beings are always collectively and personally creating meanings which affect futures. A solid friendship involves the very same process. To honor each other's otherness as well as celebrating shared meanings, two persons must speak freely and listen well to each other. As they do so, both of them will be different because of their conversation. Authentic conversation always involves the co-creation of selves. Such a relationship will move in ways that neither could have fully envisaged at the start, because it will have to take into account both friends' horizons. To put it differently: the personal and relational possibilities that stretch out in front of any friendship will inevitably be in very important ways the joint creation of the conversation between the friends.[14]

Conversation in this sense never means idle or random chatter, although it can be quite playful at times. Rather, conversation names the ongoing encounter of the "facts" of one life with the "facts" of another, of the "facts" of one people with the "facts" of other peoples. Such an encounter helps to create the future forms of the relationship and the personal and group identities involved. The ongoing conversation about "the facts" which constitutes our public world is analogous to that of friendship, but is of course profoundly more complicated.

An intentional Christian community is intent upon the public implications of the lively conversation in its midst between the Christian "fact" and the "facts" of its immediate cultural situation.[15] Recall once again that what we have called an "intentional community" in this book is a group of people that has some characteristics of both the *primary* group (e.g., affective bonding, voluntary membership, commitment to remaining in relationship) and the *secondary* group or formal organization (e.g., tasks to accomplish, a division of work, feedback on its performance). Let's pursue these two dimensions again for a moment as a way of introducing the necessarily intertwined themes of this chapter and the next.

The particular kind of reflective, action-oriented conversation called intentional Christian community offers its members a model for the community's internal life by keeping a steady focus on the quality of mutuality among and between members which is necessary if intentional community is to survive and thrive. In this chapter we are especially interested in how persons who are part of our American "fact," with its heavily individualistic bent can be together mutually in the light of the Christian "fact," with its communitarian orientation.[16] Our name for a way of being together which respects both our uniqueness and our relatedness is *mutuality*. In mutuality the dangerously liberating memories and transformative hopes of the Christian tradition are embodied in a mode of being together with others, a particular form of solidarity. Mutuality is the internal edge of the conversation which is intentional Christian community.

Intentional Christian communities also offer their members a way of collectively engaging the surrounding social and cultural world. In Chapter Four we noted how intentional communities in America are affected by the particular systems world which surrounds them; in Chapter Six we will focus on how such communities can become actively engaged in the ongoing creative transformation of their society and culture. Social and cultural engagement is the external edge of intentional Christian community.

We have *not* just described a "private" and a "public" side of the lives of intentional Christian communities. Both dimensions are profoundly public.[17] How we are with one another in our immediate relationships both nurtures and limits the quality of our presence in the world; how we are in the world and the world in us cannot fail to condition our communal relationships in quite profound ways. Participation in an intentional Christian community always entails both kinds of promise, both kinds of commitment. The members of every authentic intentional Christian community have a mission of *koinonia* and *diakonia* to one another *and* to the larger world within which their community lives, moves and has its being. Intentional Christian community is an ongoing, double-edged conversation.

We will spend considerable time in this chapter taking a practical approach to the development of mutuality within intentional Christian communities. We offer no apologies for doing so. Along the way it will probably occur to you that authentic mutual relationships make sense for all persons, not merely for Christians. Any authentic version of human relationships does indeed require an adequate level of mutuality among those involved. But in an intentional Christian community, the "why" of mutuality is of paramount concern. It was clear to Jesus, through his own experience of God as his Father, that as sisters and brothers all of us are to be united in a discipleship of equals. This is an ultimate reason for members of a Christian community to live together in mutuality. And an ultimate reason is a religious reason.[18]

A second point regarding our presentation of mutuality must be made. An authentically mutual way of relating is something which the members of intentional Christian communities must aspire to build together, rather than a prerequisite for beginning an intentional Christian community. The description of mutual relationships to follow therefore has the character of an ideal, although we hope a very practical one. Any intentional Christian community, like any friendship or marriage, will fail at times against its commitment to mutual relations; an intentional Christian community which fails consistently to establish a climate of mutuality among its members, cannot validly claim the title of "community."

"One Body in Christ and Members of One Another"

Every contemporary Christian community is part of an ancient and ongoing conversation in which the Christian "fact" speaks to the present generation and is spoken to by it. That ongoing conversation is what we sometimes call "tradition." It is easy to forget just how ancient a conversation our tradition is. The specifically Christian form of it is, of course, nearly 2,000 years old, but when we remember that Jesus was always and only a Jew, we begin to realize that the conversation that intentional Christian communities are part of is something far older than two millennia.[19]

It is in the context provided by this ancient and ongoing religious conversation that the deepest significance of mutuality in intentional Christian communities is revealed. When we read the Christian "fact" faithfully, we recognize that while mutuality is always the kind of social and psychological reality that we are about to explore in this chapter, it is never only that. How we are together in the world with other persons is for Christians also a matter of religious, i.e., ultimate, significance. Members of intentional Christian communities are called by an authentic reading of their own tradition to take mutual relationships in community life with ultimate seriousness. The Christian "fact" requires this of us. Let's explore that requirement.

In many ways, the following account of mutuality is a description in contemporary language of the ancient awareness that relationships must embody certain qualities if they are to bear good fruit. Chief among these qualities is equal respect and care for one's own experience and that of others. To comport ourselves with such respect in our everyday lives together is to be mutual. It is one crucial expression of loving our neighbors as we love ourselves.[20] For Jews and Christians such love is at the same time the primary symbol of our covenantal relationship with a God who loves us. The authentic religious heritage of Judaism and Christianity is primarily a communal and not an individualistic one. It shows how we are to be *together* in the world, not just how to be good individuals. It reminds us that "who is my neighbor?" is our most fundamental kind of question. It may be fairly noted that our Jewish sisters and brothers have remained more faithful to the fundamentally communal character of our common religious heritage than most western Christians have.

Since mutuality is one of the four requisite dimensions of intentional Christian community, a group that fails to establish adequately mutual relations will be quite limited *qua community*. What we mean to say is that mutuality is not an extra or frosting on the cake called intentional community. It is one of four essential ingredients in the cake's recipe. Mutuality is our name for how people *must* communicate with one another if the reality called intentional Christian community is to emerge among them in vital form — if, in the ancient Pauline language of our tradition, the People of God are to become "one body in Christ and members of one another." When Paul offers directives about the truth that must characterize relationships, about handling anger and grudges, about the kind of language we ought to use in speaking to one another, about gentleness and patience, he is not speaking only of good community dynamics, but of "the way you have learned from Christ," of "the one Body and one Spirit," of "the peace that binds you together." He is speaking of ultimate realities.[21] We become the People of God as we become One Body.

That there is a crucial connection between the quality of mutuality — of "one bodyness" — in Christian community and the ongoing creative transformation of community members and their world is one of the central assumptions of our religious tradition. This strong Jewish and early Christian emphasis on the social or relational character of being human has been dangerously eroded in modern Western culture. We saw the American version of this erosion in our exploration of the individualism of contemporary American culture. It is also apparent in the widespread modern privatization of religion ("The *only* important question is: Have *I* accepted Jesus Christ as my *personal* savior?") We have come to live as if we first exist and then form relationships.

But our individual and collective identities do not exist prior to our relationships; they arise continually out of them. The web of relations out of which we emerge initially and from which we continue to emerge from day to day for the balance of our lives is our perpetual womb. Our relations are constitutive of our selves. Just and loving selves can only be born out of relational webs which nurture justice and love, however imperfectly. The social bodies of which we are a part continually form us and are formed by us. Personhood is always a relational or social matter. As in our example of friendship above, all our relationships are co-creative events in which we contribute to the identities and therefore the possibilities of one another for better and for worse.

Within an intentional Christian community which is consistently committed to becoming one body in its praxis of mutuality:

— Every act of authentic self-disclosure makes one person's story a gift to the becoming of another.

— Every act of genuine understanding of another's story enhances the size of the listener's spirit.

— Every act of responsible challenge in the spirit of understanding is an invitation to an increase in stature.

— Every act of non-defensive exploration in response to challenge reflects a commitment to a life of larger dimensions.

Any intentional Christian community which struggles to develop the discipline and tenderness and resilience of spirit that such giving and receiving demand, will know at first hand the moments of dying entailed and the intensity of living that arises out of such acts.[22] To care for each other and accept each other's care in this spirit of deeply paschal mutuality is to place the relational events of everyday community life in the ultimate context of love. It is to become one body. It is to reenact in present relationships the dangerous memory of Jesus' love.

To abide with others in love is to abide in genuine mutuality. And intentional Christian community is a place where such abiding is cherished and nurtured. It is an ongoing forming of one body. Within intentional Christian community, mutuality is the fundamental and concrete expression of Christian *koinonia* and *diakonia*, and the community's eucharistic meal is the primordial symbol of that common fellowship of mutual service. Within intentional Christian community, fidelity to a mutual way of being-together-in-the-world becomes a sacred obligation.

Dimensions of Mutuality

We have seen that in the "hybrid" social form called intentional community, a balance must be established and faithfully maintained between concerns having to do with the quality of our being-together within the community and those having to do with the quality of our acting-together in our larger world. It is precisely when intentional communities help their members creatively to connect these interrelated dimensions of our world that they function as mediating structures.

We are addressing ourselves in this chapter to an aspect of a community's life which is particularly crucial for the "primary-group" dimension of the life of intentional communities — the quality of mutuality in interpersonal relationships among community members. As you begin to explore this foundational dimension of community life more thoroughly, two important cautions are in order. First, intentional Christian communities do not begin with a fully adequate version of such relationships, nor is any community perfectly consistent in its practice of mutuality. This way of relating is both a goal to which community members deliberately aspire and a way of being together which matures over time. Second, mutuality should not be equated with intimacy or intensity of relationship. Mutual give and take is possible and important in routine transactions, as well as being essential for deeper ones. The members of some small communities will choose to stress the primary group aspect of community life; relationships among them will tend in the direction of greater intensity. Other communities will focus primary attention on the task which they wish to pursue together; their interpersonal closeness will be more limited. But the pattern of relationship negotiated by community members must be adequately mutual if community is to survive and thrive among them.

The Four Moments of Mutuality

The basic relational option facing members of intentional community is that of mutual vs. non-mutual relating. Relationships within community are non-mutual when we are unable to let others know about our point of view appropriately or when we let our frame of reference and agenda be the only, or at least the most important, one involved in communication with others.

By *mutuality* we mean the capacity of persons to share their perceptions, feelings, wants, needs, beliefs and knowledge appropriately with each other, and to understand accurately and respect the differences that exist among them as these emerge in the community's conversation.[23]

In mutual relationships within intentional community, persons engage in direct and non-manipulative interaction, with each attempting to understand and respect the frame of reference of others; controlling and being-controlled are rejected as ways of being in relationship; disagreement and conflict call for genuine negotiation; and consensus among respectful equals becomes the preferred mode of making communal decisions.

In order for mutuality to characterize relationships among a community's members, those involved must be able and willing to do four things:

1) tell their own stories, including the accompanying feelings

2) understand accurately the events and feelings of other members' stories

3) give constructive positive and negative feedback to members of the community at appropriate moments

4) receive feedback from others with a measure of openness.

Disclosure, empathy, giving feedback and receiving feedback are thus the four basic moments of mutuality in communal conversation. Together they constitute the necessary everyday way of communicating together in authentic intentional community. Please note the word "necessary" in the previous sentence. Without an adequate level of mutuality in its ongoing conversation, a group should not call itself a community. Note also that the other three core dimensions of intentional community discussed in this book—engagement with the world, networking and ongoing conversation with the Christian "fact"—are likewise necessary conditions. Considered alone each of these four aspects is a necessary but not sufficient condition for authentic Christian intentional community; taken together they *constitute* such a community.

The Two Levels of Mutuality

The four moments of mutuality can be thought of as involving two basic levels. Disclosure and accurate empathetic understanding constitute the primary level of mutuality in relationships between and among persons. At this level most of the time I will tell you where I am as regards the issue at hand appropriately and directly; you will understand my disclosure from my point of view and indicate your understanding to me. Most of the time you will say where you are and I will receive your statement accurately.[24]

These reciprocal behaviors feed on each other. If you want to encourage me to tell you where I stand, one effective way is to give me access to your position and experience. If I want you to understand me from my perspective, I can try to walk in your shoes for a time. Engaging in these reciprocal behaviors consistently establishes a level of basic decency, trust and care in human relationships. This is the basic or foundational level of mutuality.

Giving feedback and being receptive to it constitute the deeper level of mutuality in relationships between and among persons. At this deeper level of mutuality, most of the time I will share my interpretation of a situation, of your behavior or of events in our relationship appropriately and directly; you will consider what I am saying with genuine openness *prior* to deciding whether you agree with my view. Most of the time you will be willing to give me similar feedback and I will receive it as a gift for my consideration.[25]

Like self-disclosure and empathy, the giving and receiving of feedback also reinforce each other. If you want me to give you clear, direct and specific feedback it will help if you can offer such feedback to me. If I want you to take my feedback on board openly, I will try to do the same with your feedback to me. Engaging in these reciprocal behaviors consistently and well makes our relationship one of significant belonging and mutually creative transformation.[26]

We describe the first level of mutuality as basic, because engaging in it is what makes it possible to move on to the deeper level. If we want our communal reelationships to grow to the deeper level of mutuality, we must consistently cultivate the first. For example, if you want me to take your feedback with openness, be sure that I have experienced your understanding. In the primary level of mutuality we demonstrate basic respect and care for each other; in the secondary level we invite each other to ongoing creative transformation. Engaging consistently in primary level mutuality earns us the right to move to deeper levels of conversation.

The notion of four moments points out the building blocks of genuine mutuality. The concept of two levels helps us to see mutuality as a dynamic process at work between and among persons.

The Requisites of Mutuality

If the members of an intentional Christian community are to move toward mutuality in their life together, five interrelated factors must come into play: self-esteem, working knowledge, skills, values and norms. The absence of any of these factors is sufficient to account for a lack of mutuality within the community's web of relationships; the presence in some degree of all of them is the bedrock of vital and creative conversation in intentional community. Let's examine each of them in turn.

Self-esteem

By "self-esteem" we mean a self-concept characterized by a realistic awareness and acceptance of one's gifts and limitations.[27] A community member with a very negative image of herself or himself is unlikely to risk the exposure and vulnerability that inevitably comes with mutuality. While he or she may deeply desire close and creative relationships with others, the instinct to protect a fragile self is likely to block attempts to draw close within community. Damaged self-esteem can be related to unresolved losses from early life including shame, abuse or abandonment, or to traumas of adult life.[28]

Self-esteem can also be diminished because a person sees herself or himself as lacking in skills for relating to others. In such instances, the opportunity to develop more adequate communication skills in community interaction or elsewhere can itself contribute to self-esteem. In fact this opportunity is one of the richest that intentional community offers its members. We will examine how this can occur in the section on skills below.

There are other instances in which the historical damage to someone's self-esteem may have been so great that their unconscious won't let them draw close enough to others to risk being wounded again. While participation in an intentional community may have many healing effects, intentional communities are not therapeutic communities and their members should be mindful of the distinction. No matter how genuine and loving a community, some wounds may call for professional care. In those instances, the role of the community is to be a group of concerned and appropriately involved persons — no more and no less.

In the absence of adequate self-esteem in the membership of an intentional Christian community, the group's efforts to establish a climate of mutuality in its relations will prove futile. When community members are being together in fidelity to the Christian narrative, the enhancement of self-esteem is a likely grace.

Working Knowledge

Any information that helps us to behave competently in particular situations can be termed "working knowledge."[29] In the case of building mutual community relationships, working knowledge is any information that helps me to understand the four component moments of mutuality so that I can engage in them effectively. This chapter, and indeed much of this book, offers working knowledge about participation in intentional Christian communities.

For example, research has shown that empathy — the capacity to appreciate the events and feelings of another's story — has two components: recognition and acknowledgement.[30] Recognition refers to hearing accurately what someone is saying and sensing accurately how he or she seems to feel about it. Acknowledgement means letting the other know that she or he has been heard accurately. Without both of these components, empathetic understanding — one of the four basic building blocks of mutuality — is not adequately present in a community's conversation.

This kind of information becomes working knowledge when it begins to influence my actions. It is one thing to understand the theory of accurate empathy. It is another to understand it in such a way that I can embody it in my concrete life with other persons.

A wide variety of excellent material of a working-knowledge sort is available in the area of interpersonal communication. Some of the best of these are included in the annotated list of suggested readings at the end of this chapter. Members of intional communities can develop their working knowledge regarding mutuality individually or in collaborative study, discussion and practice.

Skills

A skill may be defined as a specific behavior or set of behaviors that can be called upon by individuals at will and in the appropriate context.[31] While working knowledge refers to what one knows, skills refer to what one can do. I may, for example, have a valid understanding of the distinction described above between recognition and acknowledgement in accurately understanding another's disclosure. It does not follow, however, that I will be able to engage in the behaviors of recognizing and acknowledging in my relationships in community life.

Over the last 20 years, a good deal of effort has been given to specifying the skills required for effective communication and to developing a method for training people in them. This method is sometimes referred to as a "micro-skills" training approach, because it takes communication as a whole and breaks it down into important components which are then taught one by one.[32]

A typical micro-skills training session would involve the following steps:

1) The instructor would give a clear definition, description and examples of the micro-skill to be learned.

2) The skill would be modeled for the students by the instructor.

3) Each student would practice the skill in an actual exchange in a group with two other persons.

4) The students would receive feedback on their practice attempts from the instructor and other participants.

5) The training group would recycle through the micro-training process until a satisfactory level of skill development begins to occur.

Members of an intentional community can work on their communication skills individually or collaboratively. Without an adequate base of skills, intentional communities cannot reach a creative level of mutuality in their shared life.

Personal Values

A personal value is a moral or ethical belief which actually influences my actions.[33] It may happen that members of a community do not engage in effective mutual communication, even when they apparently have the self-esteem, working knowledge and skills to do so. In such instances it is possible that the persons involved do not judge such communication to be essential at the level of values. When might this happen in community life?

In certain intentional communities, members may assume that their strong common commitment to social justice, educating students, caring for the sick, feeding the poor, or working for peace will somehow insure that they communicate effectively and mutually. Different preferences, priorities and sensibilities within the community will somehow "all be worked out." All that really matters is why the community has come together. The assumption is that common commitment will see the group through the everyday tasks of setting and pursuing common goals.

In a variation on this theme, one sometimes hears that adequate communication in intentional communities will take care of itself because "we're all Christians here." This would imply that Christians are somehow absolved of the hard work of establishing a climate of mutuality in their conversation.

The hard fact is that many, if not most, intentional communities begin with a high degree of commitment but fail precisely because their members are unable or unwilling to build a relational foundation of mutuality adequate to sustain the ongoing life of the community. As will be apparent from this chapter, there is nothing automatic or magical about mutuality and how it comes about. And there are no supernatural remedies for intentional communities, Christian or otherwise, which fail at this fundamental task.

An early necessity in the life of an intentional community is for members to clarify together their values and expectations with regard to the quality and depth of their communication with each other. Some important questions in this regard are:

— To what extent is mutuality a value for the particular people in this community?

— Are we willing to invest the required time and energy in nurturing this dimension of our life together?

— How will we do so, concretely and specifically?

Cultural and Institutional Norms

A final factor that influences the quality of mutuality within intentional community focuses not on what individuals bring to their relationships, but on the norms or rules of the larger settings within which the community is situated.[34] We have already looked, for example, at norms in U.S. culture. Do you see how such norms might affect the practice of mutuality within intentional Christian communities in our country?

In a profoundly individualistic culture like the American one, particularly in the middle-class version examined in Chapter Three, religion has tended to shape and be shaped in an individualistic direction. Without denying a role for participation in a congregation or community, American religiousness has tended to move toward a "me-and-God," private, vertical and supernatural spirituality.[35] This normative cultural understanding of religiousness has inevitably left its mark on our sense of right relationships in community as well. Let's look at two examples.

We might sometimes find ourselves trying to resolve conflict with others in community chiefly through private prayer and symbolic gestures, perhaps attempting, for example, to deal with our anger at someone in community by suppressing it and offering her or him a gesture of peace at liturgy. But if true peace among us has in fact been broken, such actions alone can become ways of avoiding the frightening and challenging demands of genuine reconciliation. It might well be better simply to say: "I can't honestly embrace you right now. Let's talk soon about what's wrong between us." And then show up for the meeting! In the light of all we have said so far about mutuality and whence it comes, we hope it is abundantly clear that any intentional Christian community is far better off if its members show up for such meetings with decent mutuality skills and habits.

A second example of norms in our religious culture which operate against mutuality involves men and women who were prepared for and later took religious vows. For many generations, seminary and convent formation included an explicit proscription of what were called "particular friendships." While this prohibition was probably intended to discourage the kind of exclusive pairing-off which often does detract from community life, it seems to have had the effect for a time of discouraging close friendships between people.

There is a serious problem here. What was then called "particular friendship" sounds very much like what we now call "intimacy" and view as an essential requirement for healthy development.[36] We have also come to recognize that creative ministry is a matter of presence and closeness with others, not distance.[37] Further, we see that in Western culture generally, the most typical time for persons to be wrestling with intimacy as a primary developmental task is during late adolescence and early adulthood — the very time when persons in religious formation were once discouraged from forming such relationships.[38] One outcome of this historical process which remains with us today is that many persons engaged in ministry and church leadership had inadequate models and mentors in the areas of mutuality and intimacy during the course of their own development. And while it is certainly the case that intimacy work can be accomplished in places other than formation programs and at times other than one's 20s, the fact remains that no mentor gives what she or he did not receive from someone.

Priests, sisters and brothers today are challenged to see celibacy and intimacy as requiring rather than contradicting each other. A new norm in this area has been emerging over the past 20 years. The transformation of longstanding cultural or institutional norms is always gradual. People who were guided by people who were guided by people who were guided by people who were strongly formed to avoid close personal connections will understandably struggle with mutuality should they find themselves trying to participate fully in the life of intentional Christian communities.[39] If, as is often the case, these persons are designated leaders in such communities, one real danger is that their felt (or unfelt) anxieties regarding mutuality and closeness will be unduly influential in "norming" the community's effort toward mutual relations. This danger can be offset as members begin to recognize that leadership within intentional community is a relational or communal event rather than a designated leader's personal prerogative. We will take up the issue of leadership's role in fostering a sense of inclusion and closeness among community members in the final chapter of this book.

Institutional norms like the two discussed here can interfere with the development of adequate levels of mutuality within intentional communities despite the presence of adequate self-esteem, working knowledge, skills and values on the part of community members. An intentional Christian community that wishes to grow toward mutuality must be prepared to heighten its awareness of the functioning of such norms and to challenge them appropriately when they are discovered.

Learning Mutuality in Intentional Communities

The members of an intentional community will have different strengths and weaknesses as mutual communicators. Some will be excellent listeners, others will have the gift of articulating their experience so concretely that they are readily understandable. Some members will be able to challenge others in the community strongly and respectfully; others will receive feedback gracefully and creatively. The gifts for mutuality among us differ.

As participants in intentional community we can become better communicators because our community serves as a kind of "modeling network" wherein we can observe good communicators in action, practice our own skills, and receive support and feedback as we do so. There are also a rich variety of training programs in communications skills available outside of communities themselves. Skills learned there can be brought back to enrich the lives of all members of the community. As a creatively functioning intentional Christian community becomes one body in the depth of its mutuality, that is precisely what happens: gifts multiply!

Every human group is composed of persons with particular strengths and weaknesses as mutual communicators. As we participate in various groups in our everyday lives, our communication skills may develop or diminish, but whatever happens in that regard is ordinarily haphazard. By contrast, the shared life of intentional Christian community offers an ongoing experiential location wherein the skills for mutuality of every member, and therefore the overall depth and quality of mutuality of the entire community, can be deliberately and systematically enhanced. Intentional communities that are working are also learning communities that are working.

Mutuality and Trust

Trust in relationships between and among members of an intentional Christian community is both a cause and an effect of mutuality. A kind of basic trust is required before we will risk disclosing ourselves to others; disclosing ourselves to others is one important factor in building trust among us. If the basis for trust inside us as individuals and among us as community members is quite limited, our capacity to let ourselves be known in community will be similarly limited. There is no more adequate way to build trust among us than to foster mutuality among us.

Ghosts in the Intentional Community

Every member of an intentional community has a history of relationships with significant persons — parents, teachers, religious leaders, etc. For better and for worse we carry the effects of those relationships into our life with others now. These absent others regularly appear like ghosts to haunt and contaminate our contemporary relationships, especially with loved ones and persons of authority. By "there-and-then" relating we mean communication between persons which is systematically distorted by unfinished emotional business from their relational histories.

There-and-then relating has a more technical name: *transference*.[40] In transferential relating, our reaction to another is so dominated by the effects of relationships from our past, especially with our parents or other figures of authority from the period of our childhood and adolescent dependency, that our current reaction to someone has little or no relationship to what she or he is actually feeling, thinking and doing here and now. In such relating we unconsciously misidentify others present now with someone who loomed large in our history. In transferential moments our past, rather than the here-and-now uniqueness of someone else, determines what their presence in our life can and cannot mean to us.

Contrary to the popular belief that such relating is sick or crazy, it is now widely recognized that all of us participate in there-and-then relating to some extent in our contemporary relationships. Transference is in fact one of three basic forms of systematic distortion which take place to some degree in all relationships between and among human beings. Along with ideology and cultural prejudices, transference is at the root of much of the destructiveness of human society and history. At the core, each is a form of systematic distortion of our relationships which limits or destroys mutuality among us. As pervasive features of all human relationships, these failures of mutuality always infect intentional Christian communities in some measure.

In transference our response to other members of our community gives them power over our sense of self-esteem and limits our options for possible action. Let's look at an example:

> A community member listens to the leader's critique of his committee's proposal regarding Advent liturgy. He experiences strong feelings of self-doubt and embarrassment, although no specific comments are directed to him.

> Later, he exclaims angrily to a friend: "Where does she get off with that high-and-mighty routine! We're not kids to be led around by the nose. I've about had it with the whole Church scene!"

In order for the distortion of here-and-now events called transference to occur within intentional community, a particular set of interpretive events must unfold. First, what another community member does to us, their manner, or the position which they hold, must resemble events that happened to us there and then (In the above example, the community leader is an authority figure). Second, we must "miss" the differences that are always present between the situation there and then and the one here and now (As an adult in a community of equals, the member in our example is not a dependent child, and the leader is not a parent). Third, we must interpret the other's response primarily as a reaction to us rather than as an expression of their experience or shortcomings (Were the leader's comments on the liturgy proposal constructive feedback from her perspective or impatient personal criticism?). Finally, our experience here and now must be primarily reactive to the other's "appraisal" of us, rather than reflecting our own authentic and differentiated response to what is transpiring in the present moment (The member became so caught up in the leader's feedback that he was not only unable to focus on liturgical planning, but felt the impulse to leave the church).[41]

Why all this talk about there-and-then relating in a book on intentional communities? As we have already noted, the Christian tradition, like its Jewish progenitor, is fundamentally communal in character: our task is to make of the world one body.[42] Anything that breaks up the body is antithetical to the fundamental Christian stance. Simply put: transference is one of the most significant barriers to authentic, mutual interaction within small communities. As such, it regularly breaks up the body of intentional Christian communities. "Mutuality" and "transference" are thoroughly contemporary ways to name, first, the Christian task of building one body, and, second, one radical barrier to the successful carrying out of that task.

The four-step process of there-and-then or transferential relating described above is especially likely to occur in intentional communities around issues of authority and power.[43] This makes both formal and informal leadership situations within intentional communities a kind of breeding ground for transference. All of us are susceptible to laying unfinished business with parents and other authority figures at the feet of those trying to lead us here and now. This is not to say that anger or hurt as a response to the behavior of persons in authority is inevitably transferential. Sometimes it's perfectly appropriate! While there-and-then relating can occur among community members in connection with any specific issue, power and authority questions are especially tricky ones from the standpoint of transference.

Unresolved transference issues constitute the most formidable barrier standing between spouses and intimate friends, because in drawing especially close to others our unfinished emotional business will inevitably be stirred up and transferred to them. Like marriage and intimate friendship (although as we have noted repeatedly, not exactly like either) intentional community requires that we draw close to others. And that is precisely when there-and-then relating will sometimes emerge as a barrier to a community authentically becoming one body.

How can members deal creatively with the complex and intricate issues of transference which will inevitably emerge in the life of an intentional community? First, members can develop their personal awarenesses of repeating patterns in how they tend to get here-and-now people mixed up with there-and-then events. Some helpful "diagnostic" questions would be:

— What sorts of persons or statements in the community tend to scare me, hurt my feelings or make me mad?

— How do I deal with such feelings when they arise?

— Are there moments when the intensity of my reactions seem somehow out of proportion in the immediate situation?

—How do I deal with leadership moves within the community?

Second, members can explore the connection between such hurtful and angry moments in the community's life and the pattern of events which was typical in their families-, churches- and schools-of-origin. This involves systematic reflection on our early experience with parents, siblings, teachers, ministers, etc. When patterns of neglect, harshness, shame, control or abuse occurred there, emotional residuals of those experiences cannot fail to condition our expectations and perceptions in community life. The critical questions are: How is here and now like there and then? How is it different?[44]

In discussing self-esteem we noted that intentional communities should not try to function as therapeutic communities.

This is true of transference issues as well. Anyone's history of woundedness from significant relationships of the past will inevitably be painfully touched from time to time if she or he risks drawing close to others in intentional community. But such wounds are not necessarily resolveable within the life of the community itself. Often enough, it will be important to work through such issues and feelings in a therapeutic relationship outside the community. In such instances a community can be a group of concerned and supportive persons as one of its members works to liberate his or her heart and head from the heavy hand of formative conversations of the past.

Fidelity to the obligations of *koinonia* and *diakonia* among members of an intentional Christian community is embodied in the quality and consistency of mutuality among us. This is how we become one body and members of one another within the community. It is how we honor the challenging memory of the Christian story in face-to-face community relationships while letting that story form the future of those primary communal bonds.

Our conviction is that intentional Christian communities have a contribution to make to the social reconstruction of U.S. culture, and that a heightened degree of mutuality among us is one side of that contribution. The dignity of the individual is rightly held sacred in our American story. Mutuality is a way of being in relationship which embodies genuine respect for the integrity, uniqueness and freedom — the individuality — of every person. It does so by not disconnecting us from each other so that we can each do our own completely individualistic thing, but rather by offering us a way of being together that respects the web of social relationships which alone nurtures authentic individuality. Wherever mutual relationships flourish in our culture, the overly individualistic version of our American story is creatively transformed. In the process relational, but not ontological, individualism is nurtured. Let us turn now to a discussion of the other side of the transformative public conversation which is intentional Christian community: awareness of and engagement with the larger social and cultural world.

Additional Resources

Mutuality: Working Knowledge and Skills

Gerard Egan offers a practical, skills-based approach to building mutual relationships in *Interpersonal Living* (Monterey: Brooks/ Cole, 1976). It offers not
only good working knowledge about the skills of mutuality, but also a set of exercises designed to help persons who want to build those skills. Members of intentional communities wishing to work collaboratively on building communications skills will find chapters 12 ("Group-specific Skills"), 13 ("The Open Group")
and 14 ("Changing Your Interpersonal Behavior") of particular interest. *Interpersonal Living* is most suitable for persons with some college background. It
includes standard references to studies of various aspects of human communication.

You & Me (Monterey: Brooks/Cole, 1977) is a "translation" of *Interpersonal Living* into somewhat simpler language. In this version, Egan has removed all references to scientific studies of communication. It is easily readable by persons
with a high school education.

A training manual authored by Michael Cowan, Gerard Egan & Maureen Bacchi, which is coordinated with *Interpersonal Living* and *You & Me*, is available
at no charge from the publisher for groups who order multiple copies of either
text. The manual contains step-by-step training exercises in all the communication skills covered in the texts. Taken together, either book and the accompany-
ing manual make up a complete training program in basic mutuality skills.

Self-esteem and our systems-of-origin

Augustus Y. Napier & Carl Whitaker recount one family's experience in family
therapy in *The Family Crucible* (New York: Bantam, 1978). The authors weave
together the story of the family's struggles and informative explanations of
what's going on from a family-systems and family-of-origin perspective. Members of intentional communities who wish to become informed about how transference issues are operating among them will benefit from a shared reading of
and coversation about this lively and informative text.

Virginia Satir's *Peoplemaking* (Palo Alto: Science and Behavior Books, 1972) is
a readily accessible and widely read primer about family life and its effects on
individual persons. Its chapters on self-worth, patterns of communication, rules
and open vs. closed systems will be of particular interest to members of intentional communities who want to pay attention to such things in their community's ongoing conversation. *Peoplemaking* will help communities to reflect back
to their familial beginnings and forward to patterns in their relationships with
one another here and now.

With the help of both of these texts it is also quite easy to draw analogies between the effects of our experiences in families-of-origin and other important
systems-of-origin such as our parishes, schools, neighborhoods and culture.
These reflections can also help intentional community members to deal with
transferential unfinished business among them.

Negotiation and conflict

A practical and principled model of negotiation is presented by Roger Fisher and William Ury in *Getting to Yes* (Boston: Houghton Mifflin, 1981). Readers of this book will find its philosophy and method to be quite consistent with the emphasis on mutuality which we have stressed in this chapter. Negotiation is a constant and ongoing process in the life of an intentional community; it is not called for only in situations of conflict. Indeed, good negotiation skills within a community can minimize unnecessary conflicts.

Becoming one body

In *Becoming Human Together* (Wilmington: Glazier, revised edition, 1982), Jerome Murphy-O'Connor deals with the explicity religious character of intentional Christian community from the perspective of Pauline pastoral anthropology, and does so in a clear and prophetic style. This text is capable of generating rich and challenging conversation among members of intentional communities who want to keep track of the religious ground of their experience in community. It also speaks forcefully of the inevitably countercultural dimension of Christian community in the modern world.

Notes

1. The connection between western culture and the symbolic structures of the Christian tradition is richly explored in part II of Bernard E. Meland, *Faith and Culture* (Carbondale: Southern Illinois University, 1953), and Northrop Frye, *The Great Code* (San Diego: Harcourt, 1983).

2. On the irreducible diversity of human cultures, cf. Clifford Geertz, "The Impact of the Concept of Culture on the Concept of Man" in *The Interpretation of Cultures* (N.Y.: Basic Books, 1973), pp. 33-54.

3. The roles of sacred symbols in all cultures is explored in "Ethos, World View and the Analysis of Sacred Symbols," Geertz, 1973, pp. 126-141. Paul Ricoeur explores the same territory from a phenomenological standpoint in *The Symbolism of Evil* (Boston: Beacon, 1969. Translated by Emerson Buchanan.) Mary Douglas likewise addresses related issues from the standpoint primarily of pre-industrial societies in *Purity and Danger* (London: Routledge & Kegan Paul, 1966), chap. 5.

4. Cf. "A New Way: Reflecting on Experience" in James E. Hug (ed.), *Tracing the Spirit* (N.Y.: Paulist, 1983), pp. 13-37.

5. "The Challenge of Peace" (Washington, D.C.: N.C.C.B., 1983), "Catholic Social Teaching and the U.S. Economy," (Washington, D.C.: *Origins*, 1985, second draft).

6. On the critical analysis of patriarchal structures, cf. Gerda Lerner's groundbreaking historical study, *The Creation of Patriarchy* (N.Y.: Oxford, 1986); the introduction and chapters 1, 3 and 4 of Elisabeth Schüssler Fiorenza, *Bread not Stone* (Boston: Beacon, 1984); and chapters 1,5 and 6 of Letty M. Russell, *Human Liberation in a Feminist Perspective*, (Boston: Beacon, 1974).

7. Critical awareness refers to our ability to be aware of the presuppositions underlying our own positions as well as those of others. It includes a sensitivity to the material and power interests which are always present in human interaction. Appreciative awareness names our capacity to appreciate the uniqueness of people, events and objects in our world from their vantage point, without merely reducing them to the categories of our current perspective. In our time the former is almost always acknowledged as important; the latter too often neglected.

For a wonderful exposition of the concept of appreciative consciousness cf. Bernard E. Meland, *Higher Education and the Human Spirit* (Chicago: University of Chicago, 1953), chap. 5.

8. David Tracy's model of theology as mutually critical correlation between faith and culture is defined in chaps. 2 and 3 of *Blessed Rage for Order* (N.Y.: Seabury, 1975). His treatment of interpretation, including theological interpretation, as conversation is to be found in chap. 3 of *The Analogical Imagination* (N.Y.: Crossroad, 1981). The latter chapter, which is entitled "The Classic," is grounded in the hermeneutical phenomenology of Heidegger, Gadamer and Ricoeur. It is a masterful statement of the necessarily interpretive or hermeneutical character of all human experience, and of how members of diverse

traditions in our irreducibly pluralistic age can deal with their interpretive differences with integrity and mutual respect.

9. That there are no uninterpreted facts is a principal aphorism of contemporary philosophical hermeneutics. The Heideggerian background of this interpretive tradition is nicely introduced in John Macquarrie, *Martin Heidegger* (Richmond: John Knox, 1968), pp. 10-41. Its full-bodied contemporary expression is succinctly presented in Robert M. Grant and David Tracy, *A Short History of the Interpretation of the Bible* (Philadelphia: Fortress, 1984. Second edition), chap. 16. The implications of the interpretive model for theological and pastoral interpretation of the scriptures today are then explored in chaps. 17 and 18 of the same text.

10. A reflection on the processive and relational character of selfhood informed by Whitehead's metaphysics can be found in Michael A. Cowan, "Emerging in Love," in Paul W. Pruyser (ed.) *Changing Views of the Human Condition* (Macon: Mercer, 1987).

11. The concept of "assumptive world" reminds us that much of what happens in human life depends on what we take for granted in making the meanings which guide our lives. Our assumptive world is the framework which makes our interpretations of life coherent. Cf. Jerome Frank, *Persuasion and Healing* (Baltimore: Johns Hopkins, 1973. Revised edition), pp. 27-35.

12. The theory of meaning being elaborated here is associated with both the American pragmatism of William James, cf. *Essays in Radical Empiricism* (N.Y.: Longmans, 1912), chaps. 1-6; and the Heideggerian interpretation of the relationship between understanding and possibility in human existence, cf. Macquarrie, 1968, pp. 10-33.

13. The pervasively interpretive character of human experience is what the metaphor of the "hermeneutical circle" names. In succinct form it reminds us that any interpretation depends on the interpreter's historical vantage point *and* that ongoing interpretation is always transforming the very vantage point from which it occurs. The "hermeneutical circle" is a metaphor for the inevitably historical, interpretive character of the human condition.

14. For a further development of the analogy of friendship to interpretation-as-conversation, cf. Bernard J. Lee, "Shared Homily: Conversation That Puts Community at Risk," *Gathering*, 1/5, 1985. The model presented by Lee is resourced in the hermeneutical theory of Paul Ricoeur.

15. A practical, pastoral version of such a model for theological reflection can be found in James D. and Evelyn Eaton Whitehead, *Method in Ministry* (N.Y.: Seabury, 1980).

16. On the communitarian character of Christian tradition from the perspective of eucharistic celebration, cf. John C. Haughey, "The Eucharist and Intentional Communities," in Bernard J. Lee (ed.), *Eucharist and Intentional Communities* (Collegeville: Liturgical Press, 1987).

17. On the public character of contemporary systematic theology, cf. Tracy, 1981, chaps. 1 and 2.

18. Through contemporary anthropological investigations we have learned that in all its diverse forms religion has a common function: to allow persons to

locate the acts of their everyday lives within an ultimate context of meaning. Cf. Geertz, 1973, pp. 98-125.

19. On taking the Jewishness of Jesus with ultimate seriousness, cf. Harvey Falk, *Jesus the Pharisee* (N.Y.: Paulist, 1985); Geza Vermes, *Jesus the Jew* (Philadelphia: Fortress, 1981); and John Pawlikowski, *Christ in the Light of Jewish Christian Dialogue* (N.Y.: Paulist, 1982).

20. On the centrality of the "double love commandment" in our religious tradition, cf. Pheme Perkins, *Love Commands in the New Testament* (N.Y.: Paulist, 1982), chap. 1.

21. Paul's letters to the Romans (12:5) and Ephesians (4).

22. The Christian tradition affirms the mystery that life comes out of death. The meaning of this theme and its profound implications for the eucharistic praxis of Christians is insightfully developed in Tad W. Guzie, *Jesus and the Eucharist* (N.Y.: Paulist, 1974), cf. pp. 87-102, 129-144 and chap. 8.

23. A skills-oriented understanding of mutuality in interpersonal relationships may be found in Gerard Egan, *Interpersonal Living* (Monterey: Brooks/Cole, 1976).

24. On the basic level of mutuality, cf. Egan, 1976, chaps. 3-8.

25. On the deeper level of mutuality, cf. Egan, 1976, pp. 155-158 and chaps. 9-11.

26. Cf. Cowan, 1987, part 5.

27. A useful exposition of self-esteem within a strong family-systems orientation can be found in Virginia Satir, *Peoplemaking* (Palo Alto: Science and Behavior Books, 1972), chap. 3.

28. On the genesis and lingering interpersonal consequences of shame, as well as the role of interpersonal bridges in its healing, cf. Gershen Kaufman, *Shame* (Cambridge: Schenkman, 1980). Such bridges and the healing associated with them are part and parcel of creative life in intentional communities.

29. On the concept of working knowledge, cf. Gerard Egan and Michael A. Cowan, *People in Systems* (Monterey: Brooks/Cole, 1979), pp 8-13.

30. On the two dimensions of accurate empathetic understanding, cf. Robert R. Carkhuff, *Helping and Human Relations* (N.Y.: Holt, Rinehart and Winston, 1969), chaps. 11 and 12.

31. For a comprehensive model of skills development, cf. Egan and Cowan, 1979, pp. 8-13 and chap. 3.

32. A set of micro-training exercises in the skills of mutuality can be found in Michael A. Cowan, Maureen Bacchi and Gerard Egan, *A Training Manual to Accompany Interpersonal Living and You & Me* (Monterey: Brooks/Cole, 1978).

33. We are here following a conception of the valuing process which includes a distinction between cognitively held values and values in use. For an extended discussion of the valuing process and its role in teaching, cf. Louis Raths, Merrill Harmin, and Sidney Simon, *Values in Teaching* (Columbus: Merrill, 1966).

34. For a clear and practical discussion of norms and how they operate

among us, cf. Prentiss L. Pemberton and Daniel Rush Finn, *Toward a Christian Economic Ethic,* (Minneapolis: Winston, 1985), chaps. 1, 8 and 9.

35. On modern religious privatism, cf. Johann Baptist Metz, *Faith in History and Society* (N.Y.: Seabury, 1980. translated by David Smith), chaps. 2 and 3. On supernaturalism, cf. Edward Schillebeeckx, *The Church with a Human Face* (N.Y.: Crossroad, 1985), pp. 4-12.

36. The classic analysis of the place of intimacy as a central developmental task in the adult life cycle is to be found in Erik H. Erikson, *Childhood and Society* (N.Y.: Norton, 1963, revised edition), pp. 263-266. Cf. also his *Insight and Responsibility* (N.Y.: Norton, 1964), chap. 4.
The religious implications of Erikson's developmental view, including his understanding of intimacy have been developed in an insightful and pastorally sensitive way by Evelyn Eaton and James D. Whitehead in *Christian Life Patterns* (N.Y.: Doubleday, 1979).

37. On intimacy and generativity, cf. Erikson, 1963, pp. 263-268.

38. On the ordinary timing of developmental tasks in our culture, cf. Erikson, 1963, pp. 269-273.

39. On developmental tasks as intergenerational phenomena, cf. Erikson, 1964, pp. 111-134. Here Erikson also conceives of developmental tasks as crises which bring the opportunity to develop personal virtues in the sense of "inherent strengths" or "active qualities." (p. 112-113).

40. A technical but readable account of transference can be found in Ralph R. Greenson, *The Technique and Practice of Psychoanalysis* (N.Y.: International Universities, 1967, volume I), chap. 3.

41. The concept of reflected appraisal is treated in Charles Horton Cooley, *Human Nature and the Social Order* (N.Y.: Schocken, 1964), chap. 5.

42. Excellent interpretations of the Pauline metaphor of "one body" can be found in Robert Banks, *Paul's Idea of Community* (Grand Rapids: Eerdmans, 1980), chap. 6, and Jerome Murphy-O'Connor, *Becoming Human Together* (Wilmington: Glazier, 1982. Revised edition), chaps. 8-11.

43. The practice of leadership and the exercise of authority in western culture has been so contaminated by the paternalism associated with patriarchal structures, that we should not be surprised if it has become a breeding ground for transference reactions. Cf. note 6 above and Richard Sennett, *Authority* (N.Y.: Vintage, 1981), chap. 2.

44. The intergenerational effects of our families-of-origin on our feelings and relationships in adult life is, along with the understanding of families as systems, at the core of contemporary understandings of human relationships and human development. For a readable account introducing this perspective, cf. Satir, 1972, and Augustus Y. Napier and Carl A. Whitaker, *The Family Crucible* (N.Y.: Bantam, 1978).
By analogy to family-of-origin perspectives and with the help of tools developed by family-of-origin therapists, members of intentional Christian communities can also reflect on the continuing effects in their lives of their experiences in churches- and cultures-of-origin.

Chapter 6

MYSTICAL POLITICISM

The Evangelization of Systems

We chose the title of this book, *Dangerous Memories*, from the work of Johannes Metz. This chapter is again deeply indebted to his reflection, especially the connection he makes between Jesus' direct and profound experience of God as his father [parent[1]], and Jesus' simultaneous recognition that the consequences of that relationship inundate all other relationships everywhere and all the time:

Following Christ always has a two fold structure. It has a mystical element and one that is situational, one that is practical and political. And in their radical nature the two do not work against each other but proportionally in step with each other. The radical nature of following Christ is mystical and political at one and the same time.[2]

We want to avoid the cliche that connecting religion and politics is but another form of liberal Christian ethics. We do not believe that this position is liberal, any more than we believe that reli-

146

gion disconnected from politics is conservative. That, too, would be a cliche. Mystical politicism is our attempt to articulate an intrinsic relationship between religion and politics. For things to be internally related they must, of course, be non-identical. Making religion and politics identical is an error not only for clerics and religious but for any Christian. Neither, however, can the necessary, internal relationship between them be denied, nor the behaviors that are consequent upon their essential connectedness. Let us look at the teaching of Jesus in the setting of the world in which he lived, and then we will make some correlations with contemporary systems intuitions.

Jesus in the Context of His World

If we want to hear accurately what Jesus teaches, we must allow his voice to speak out of its own world: a Middle Eastern world, a thoroughly semitic world, an ancient world.

Within the Hebrew people themselves, there was a profound sense of interconnectedness.[3] Recall that God's covenant with Abraham was in fact a covenant with a people (all Abraham's descendants), and that this same covenant had effects on all the tribes of the earth who are to honor Abraham (Gen. 12:1-9). If there is a people in the world with whom God has an agreement, then all other peoples' interaction with that people will be affected by that agreement, for we are all co-habitants of the same earth-home. There is no such thing as a relationship with one individual that is without effects in other parts of the relational web.

In the Hebrew experience, members of a tribe are so interconnected that when a good thing that happens to one it happens to all, as with Abraham. And when one member violates God's directive, the whole people suffers. Joshua cannot understand why the Hebrews' assault on the city of Ai failed. One of the men, Achan, unknown to the others, took plunder against Yahweh's instruction. Yahweh says: "Israel has sinned . . . That is why the sons of Israel cannot stand up to their foes" (Joshua 7:10-12). Achan is Israel. These Israelite persons are not individuals with separate destinies, but individuals with a corporate destiny.

Let us hear from another part of the Middle East, a treaty which a Hittite king made with three lesser lords. The treaties that each made with the king were identical and include the following provision:

> Behold, within my land are three noblemen: you, O Targashnallis, Mashhuiluwas, and Manappa-Dattas . . . The one of you is not to fall out with the other, and one should not seek to kill the other, or capture the other. And if you, Targashnallis, do evil against them, I will take their part, and you will be my enemy. But if they fall out with you, then I will take your part, and they shall be my enemies. Because I gave the same pact, be at one . . ."[4]

Connection with the king causes interconnectedness between all those connected with the king. That is what Jesus says about all people, since we are without exception "connected" with God. Given the symbiotic relationship between faith and culture, we must suppose that these relational intuitions are in the cultural air that Jesus breathes, even if those specific words do not ring in his ears. Jesus has Jewish ears. Jesus' relation to God as his father becomes the paradigm for universal interconnectedness.

Frequently in this book we have used the expressions, "relational web," "web of systems," etc., to communicate the interconnectedness of all people with each other. One way of interpreting the message of Jesus is that he sees the profound consequences of the Fatherhood (Parenthood) of God for the relational web. People are siblings for biological reasons (Mk 3:31-35; Lk 11-27-28). But because of who God is, all those who hear the Word are brothers and sisters, mothers and fathers to each other. Because of who God is, we are an eschatological family. Our eschatological familyship is a more ultimate fact about us than all our other ties. This relationship constitutes a new, all-inclusive relational web that does not eliminate roles. Proper roles illuminate, nurture, and enliven the relational web. What eschatological familyhood does is affirm proper roles, yet makes them all ultimately subordinate to the discipleship of equals among us.

For example, neighbor is no longer constituted by physical proximity. To the question, "Who is my neighbor?" Jesus answers in parable that human need makes neighbors of us all. Need puts us in each other's back yard! That is true even of those whom historical experience has labeled "bitter adversary" (Luke 10:25-37). The label is a lie: the truth is that we are sisters and brothers, each to every other. So there is no piece of the relational web, whether minisystem or megasystem, that is untouched by Jesus' experience of what God's relationship with us creates among us. That is part of Paul's commanding vision: "All of you are baptized in Christ, you have clothed yourselves in Christ: there are no more distinctions between Jew and Greek, slave and free, male and female. All of you are one in Christ Jesus" (Gal 3:27-28).

It is one of the quirks of cultural history that the Western Christological tradition has been so overly pre-occupied with the Johannine Logos/Incarnational model, that the parables and their message about how people are to be together in the world have not seriously conditioned Christological dogma.[5] We surely agree with Sallie McFague's judgment that the critical content of Jesus' parables is about our relational life with God and together among ourselves.[6] Loving God and loving one another are of a piece: the second commandment (loving each other) is like the first (loving God). Christians have that on quite high authority!

The Ecology of Relationships

Ecology is a word from our age, and could not have been part of Hebrew consciousness in the time of Jesus. The ecology of systems which we discussed in Chapter Four holds that all of us are already related. We don't become related for the first time when we become friends or spouses or co-workers. What these special relationships do is focus and heighten some of our togetherness in the world. We may not have met, but we are interdependently interrelated in multiple systems. For example, each person's car, house, methods of garbage disposal, have effects on everybody's environment, and each person's consumer habits have effects on the total economic system.

By the same token, we should not think of love as the cause of relatedness. We are already related whether we like it or not. What love does is redeem our relatedness. Nor, for that matter, does the parenthood of God cause us to be related. Rather, it transforms the total texture of our relatedness — or, to put it differently, it reconstructs our human systems. The Mystical Body does not initiate pervasive relationality. Rather it intensifies it and, above all, makes it safer and safer and safer (as the saying goes) for children and flowers.

Let us bring the ecology of relationality closer to home. Most saddened, dysfunctional, wounded persons were wounded in or by a disfunctioning system. Suppose that such a person pulls back from the system's dynamics from time to time to enter therapy. With what one learns in successful therapy, one cannot simply go back into the same system as a healed person and be there as an effective and satisfied interactor. Either the system recruits the person back into the wounded pattern; or the system changes to contain the "new" person; or finally, the healed person does not let that old system continue to be a principal identity forming context. The obvious message is that systems must be healed fully as much as individuals. A healed system is far more likely to heal a wounded member, than *vice versa*.

The Word that Jesus proclaims demands a thoroughgoing systems transformation. It may not be only that, but it is never less than that. In the Christian story, as we have already seen, natural family relationships are subsumed into the eschatological family. The basis of neighborliness is redefined. Nationality, gender identification and economic condition lose their ability ever to create ascendency. Further, the behaviors normally reserved for friends must be equally our comportment with "enemies" (Lk 6:27-35). Patriarchy is over, as is every form of domination (Mt. 23:8-10). The leader is the servant (Mk 10:41-45). Each of these directives is, of course, an unmistakable message to individual persons. But, more radically, they accost the very bases of relationality.

At the level of provocative intuition Jesus senses that the Fatherhood of God has implications for the behaviors of social systems, though surely not in concepts such as these. God as father is a root metaphor, reflecting Jesus' religious culture. Under this metaphor, Jesus explores his personal relationship with God in such depth as to offer human history a new structure of existence. He has the resources in his Jewish deep story to sense the reality of the relational web and its redemption through the Kingdom God offers, an offer that is indeed Good News. (Kingdom, as a metaphor for what God offers, is also based in Jewish religious culture in Jesus' time, and reflects the same gender bias as Father.)

When we speak of social transformation, there are two perspectives, each of which is valid. The first is that if enough individual members of a society change, the society itself is subject to social reconstruction. But we have experienced the difficulty that arises when individuals with a conversion experience try to exist within an unconverted group. Secondly, it is also true that if a system is transformed, the individuals whose identity is formed within it will be offered the gift of new life. Both approaches are always necessary. However, the better we understand the dynamics of systems, the more important does it seem to call the systems themselves to a conversion experience.

Consider, for example, this aspect of the American cultural system. In 1984, 14.5 percent of Americans were living below subsistence level—11.5 percent of whites, 28.4 percent of Hispanics, and 33.8 percent of blacks. This is true at the same time that Americans, who are about five percent of the world's population consume a disproportionately huge amount of the world's food, goods and energy. It is true at the same time that nations with lesser resources have a much smaller percentage of people who live below the poverty level. This means that there are deep problems in the complex economic systems that shape how the world's goods are distributed, whether nationally or internationally.

Now if the Gospel does as Jesus says, brings Good News to the poor, it must address cultural systems and not just individual lives. If the Good News does as Jesus says, makes no distinction between male and female, it must address cultural systems (including ecclesial systems) and not just individuals. If the Good News does as Jesus says, precludes violence as a response to disagreement, it must address megasystems and not just individuals.

During most of its existence, the church has worked at the world's transformation by calling individual persons to metanoia. Today we have recognized the necessity of calling for the conversion of systems. It is not as though the church has never until our age trafficked with politics. It has often been up to its neck in politics, internally and externally. But what we are pressing here is different: it is a deliberate, highly conscious recognition that systems themselves have a quasi-life of their own. Human beings bring systems into existence, and once they have done that, systems have their own habits of heart and action. Moreover, the habits of a system are far more tenacious than those of any individual. As Thomas Clarke argues persuasively,the evangelization of culture is possible "only through educational processes, *basically processes of community formation*, that deal seriously with the cultural captivity afflicting all of us and that offer alternative cultural ways."[7] This chapter is concerned with house churches, individually and in networks, as strategically effective processes of community formation, able to engage in the evangelization of structures.

Privatized faith is no longer an option for us, as Metz's work makes clear. He writes from a German perspective, but the privatization of religion is even more pronounced in our American culture. We have in the separation of church and state something never intended by the Constitution, whose original intent was to prevent a state religion. Privatization, as Dennis McCann and Charles Strain characterize it,

> . . . means living a kind of moral and religious schizo-phrenia, in which one's personal "inwardness" continues to respond to the conventions of Christian piety, while one's outward behavior in various social roles displays no discernible difference from that of non-believers . . . [It is] a cultural process undermining all moral and religious traditions in advanced industrial societies.[8]

Because house churches are squarely in the middle of life, encouraging and guiding our deep commitments to human history, they tend to discourage privatism. The intentional Christian community aims at solid integration of religious values and daily social behaviors. The discernible, public difference that faith makes is the palpable basis of the church as a sacrament of Christ.

Life in a First World System

In the pages of this book we are primarily concerned with house churches in the context of our American culture. For the sake of focus, let us keep in mind three systems issues that American bishops are recommending as objects of evangelization in American experience: the challenge of peace (and its relation to foreign policy); economics (and the massive effects of American economic policy on the entire world); and the role of women in our culture and our church. It is not our intention in this book to address any one of these in detail. However, for the sake of concreteness, the remainder of this chapter will largely focus on economic concerns as a concrete setting for the mystical politicization of the house churches in our land.

We shall begin with an historical reflection upon the origins of our economic system, following Metz's work.[10] After the demise of the feudal system, the industrial revolution provided a new socio-economic base for what we now count as "first world." It is characterized by a massive middle class.[11] There is no unanimous sociological or economic agreement about the exact definition of middle class. Where it begins and ends is partly a function of cultural perception. The income range of what is called middle class in our country is quite broad: popularly it excludes those below poverty level and "the very rich." For our purposes we accept the general popular perception of middle class in the United States. Even the American lower middle class has it far better than most people in the world.

This socio-economic system has been able to use its resources to produce food, energy, and goods in incredible abundance. In this country, "we" grow more wheat, corn and potatoes than "we" can use — so the government pays "us" not to plant, or buys up "the surplus." "We," "us," and "the surplus" are in quotes, because they have a quite special, limited meaning. "We" and "us" do not include all citizens of the United States. They mean "middle class and upper class." The "we" does not include a fourth of all Hispanics and a third of all Blacks in this country who live in poverty. Since these people do not have nearly enough, "surplus" cannot mean "more than all of us in this country need." Basically, "surplus" means "more than the socio-economic system managed by the middle and upper classes needs."

Obviously, we are dealing with a very complex systems issue. If the Good News of Jesus Christ is for the poor, then proclamation of this Word cannot but be addressed to socio-economic systems. And for all the reasons we have already dealt with in our discussion of mediating structures in culture, it is clear that the one who proclaims the Word to the system must itself be a smaller system, networked with other small systems, a corporate Minister of the Word, of which the intentional Christian communities are a crucial Christian instance.

There is an analogy between the poor who are excluded from the socio-economic "we" in this country and the poor in the third world. Just as profits of the vineyard owners were not shared equitably with the grape pickers in California, American multinationals (half of the multinational corporations in the world are American) have not shared profits with the people of third-world nations, from whose goods, resources and labor the multinationals make their immense profits.

In our earlier chapter on American culture, we paid careful attention to a recent study of contemporary American mores, *Habits of the Heart*. One of the criticisms that has been made of the book is that its sampling is primarily middle class, and even upper middle class, and that it has not listened adequately to the story of the poor and the disenfranchished. That is true. And that might be true also of our attention to middle-class America in this chapter. However, we are convinced that the large middle class is central to the *structure* of our socio-economic system. In many if not most instances, the poor and disenfranchised are precisely that because of this middle-class story. American mores are created largely by our middle class, which is a deeply consumerist society. These consumerist mores do not leave the poor untouched, as cars parked in front yards and TV aerials atop hungry households testify. The two of us writing this book acknowledge freely that we are middle-class Americans, a situation that profoundly shapes our perspective. We are trying to live and write from where we are and what we know.

There is a growing sense that the future of the world is going to have to look significantly different than its past if the human history is to survive. For some time now Western writers have been speaking about the end of the modern world, or the emergence of a post-modern world. Metz agrees with this judgment, and believes that "we are now living within the final phases, which is also the transitional phase, of an historical period."[12] Then he asks a very hard question: "Who is the *historical subject* of this end situation? and what processes of historical transition and revolutionary change are emerging within it?"[13] Whose world is ending?

Metz uses the French word, loaded as it has become, for a middle-class person: *bourgeois*. The bourgeoisie — we middle class — have largely been the bearers of the modern age. In answer to Metz's question, it is we middle class who are the subjects of the end. Perhaps this has a melodramatic ring to it. But the conclusion seems inevitable. In ways that were never the case before, the destiny of the world is of a piece. None of the practiced socio-economic structures of the Western world seems able to carry an intimately webbed world along on a single destiny. Something must change, and in all likelihood we are part of the something that has got to give.

We who are middle class have been born into a particular world and have been socialized effectively in its habits of heart. We have been told that God made the world good, and our enjoyment of the world has reinforced our faith: we have seen the amber waves of grain and broken the crusts of its fine breads. Enjoyment is no sin. The tragedy is that not everyone is experiencing God through the sacrament of plenty. "Yahweh Sabaoth will prepare for all peoples a banquet of rich food, a banquet of fine wines, of food rich and juicy, of fine strained wines . . . The Lord Yahweh will wipe away the tears from every cheek" (Is 25:6, 8). There is no glory in wretchedness, except perhaps when intractable forms of it evoke a greatness of spirit.

It is counter-productive to feel guilty for finding ourselves middle-class people. That makes about as much sense as feeling guilty for being native speakers of English. However, once we have understood and named the system in which we exist, along with its consequences, we are under requirement of the Good News to create a new earth.

Courting Danger

When Johannes Metz suggests that the middle class is the historical subject of the end of the modern world, he means most of us who would be reading (not to mention writing!) this book.

It is a temptation to think of house churches as built upon Christian memories that are dangerous to someone else (the multinationals, for example). Yet it is our own lifestyle that is first put at risk by genuine conversation between our social situation and the dangerous memory of Jesus the Liberator who is Good News for the poor.

Or again, responding to the bishops' pastoral on "The Challenge of Peace" is not merely dangerous to people who manage the Pentagon. War industry accounts for about 10 percent of the world's total economy,[14] and a much higher percentage in the United States. Making products for war is one of the principal structuring forces in the American economy. It is, in fact, an integral part of our entire social system. The principal and substantial income of millions of middle-class Americans depends upon this aspect of our economy. Responding seriously, systemically, and successfully to the peace pastoral would affect the income of a significant portion of us middle-class people, and would radically challenge our entire economic structure.

We have no experience of peace as a structuring force operative within our economy. Over the last several years, we have had the largest military budgets in the history of "peace" time. John Kavanaugh points (in reference to the 1981 budget) that the monies appropriated for food stamps would run the Pentagon for 33 minutes, and that all of the U.S. contributions to the United Nations (an attempt at a social structure of world peace) from 1946 through 1978 would run the Pentagon for 19 days. [15]A little over a year ago, Congress passed an appropriation of $17 million to initiate a Peace Academy. That is only impressive until we remember the $17 million represents one-fifth of the cost of a single sophisticated fighter plane — not exactly overwhelming as a serious exploration of peace as a social system. What is at stake, if should we actually cause peace? What would be endangered? For a start, the lifestyle of middle-class America would be placed in jeopardy, at least until a new peace structure could emerge.

Again, the memory of the equality of discipleship of all women and men is not dangerous only to patriarchical structures within the church and elsewhere. It is dangerous to all women and men in our culture, because it upends social structures that are pervasive. A change in *some* of the gender roles of women is a change in *all* of the system. It effects a change in gender roles for men, which in its turn reaffects the gender roles of women, etc.

The economic system which keeps the poor poor in this country and the poor even poorer in many third-world countries concretely depends for its functioning on the consumer habits of the vast American middle class. Those same habits, of course, infect the upper economic strata as well as the poor.

This is not the place for a detailed analysis of the power of American consumerism, or the power of the middle class to effect change in that system. Those are presumed. Neither of us as writers is competent to do such an analysis, and it is being done well by others.[16] Most important for the American church, however, is the Bishops' Pastoral on Economics, which could become the same kind of constitution for the American church that Medellin and Puebla have been for the Latin American church. It could become that! Whether it does or not depends upon the response of middle-class Catholics.

As Kavanagh demonstrates, "marketing and consuming infiltrate every aspect of our lives and behavior. They filter all the experience we have of ourselves."[17] We have learned to need houses with virtually unused formal living and dining rooms, as well as a large family room where most time is spent. We have one and usually more than one car (seldom those that get above 45 miles to the gallon, even though that technology is widely available). Air conditioning and heating systems that cool or heat large unused areas as well as immediately used space. Garbage disposals that facilitate disposing of much still-edible leftover food. We know these things too well to need an extended list. But we are far less conscious of the incredibly subtle and pervasive practices of advertising and marketing that socially construct us into "needers" of these products. One of the most deeply ingrained middle-class habits is upward mobility ("upward" means more financial resources, more house space, more products, more "more"). It is next to impossible in our culture for a family to say "No" to the offer of more salary and a "higher" economic status even when its present situation is already ample for a fully decent life. As difficult as that "No" is, when members of a house church all choose to change their lifestyle, the sub-culture of their *koinonia* provides a sustaining and encouraging context.

Consumerism is a way of life. It is a central aspect of our cultural system. Christians and others are beginning to recognize its shape. Social analysis helps us name our situation. As we retrieve the Judaeo-Christian conscience that no one is allowed to accumulate non-essentials until the basic needs for human dignity have been met for all our brothers and sisters in the world, we have to make up our hearts and minds to live differently. Most of the time most of us fail over and over to live differently because our environing system is without support for these countercultural intentions. We feel helpless. To be sure, it is a far different kind of helplessness than the poor of the third world feel. Nonetheless, it *is* a true helplessness that is beginning to form a basis in American culture for doing what the poor of the third world are doing: banding together for empowerment and networking with other groups for still greater empowerment. In a word, we are building mediating structures. What we cannot do alone we can often do together and only together. "Together" means community for Christians. It means *koinonia, diakonia, leitourgia,* and *kerygma* — when *kerygma* requires us to set the table for all of our brothers and sisters. We must be com-panions, bread sharers.

There are levels of poverty and kinds of helplessness in this country that are very similar to the poverty of third-world areas. The theology of liberation and ICCs on the Latin American model fit their situation. So that is one of the intentional Christian community forms that must be nourished in this country, and is in fact being nourished. Small groups of the poor and disenfranchised that link social analysis and faith are effective change agents in many parts of this country. In some of the barrios of San Antonio, for example, organized Christian groups have done many of the same things as the ICCs in Sao Paolo Brazil: had streets repaired and paved, solid but inexpensive houses built, sewage systems installed, etc. While there are some analogies with Latin American experience, basically the American socio-economic system is a middle-class system. There is a strong need, therefore, for house churches in middle-class America that can undertake some social reconstruction of our American story precisely through social reconstruction of our own middle-class story. For whether we like the sound of it or not, American culture is largely describable as middle class, and the church itself is largely middle class: these are the social facts within which our faith is contextualized.

Once we sense that in our social situation the greatest potential for calling megasystems to conversion lies with the middle class, we get a new sense of the mission of the church in this country: reconstructing our own stories. We are dealing with memories that are dangerous for us.

Our American Church in Mission

Let us try to accept "middle class" as a reasonably accurate generalization of American Catholicism, even though it is a value-laden word. Most American Catholics are, in fact, middle class, including some portion of the large Hispanic membership. Most diocesan bishops and priests, most women and men religious, and most of the new lay leadership, are products of middle-class families. The majority of our parishes minister to middle-class people. Most of our schools and universities educate middle-class people. Most of our hospitals presently serve middle-class people.

The good news is that the church is already in place where our American work needs to be done: for the middle class is precisely the place where conscientization has the best chance of engendering the social reconstruction of our American story. If the good news is that we are probably already in the right place at the right time, the bad news is that we participate so deeply in our cultural values that it is not easy for us to become prophetic to our rather comfortable selves. Religious and priests often feel guilty of being middle class, and guilt is disabling. A common response is to go somewhere else to have social effects. John Grindel has attempted to formulate a local ecclesiology for the American church:

> The Church's primary strategy for effecting [change in our socio-economic system] is through a conversion of the middle class in this country. The middle class must be the primary audience for the Church as it goes out to proclaim the Word. There are two main reasons for this. First of all, within the political and economic system of the United States it is the middle class which has the clout, the strength, the numbers to effect change within the system. In other words, they have the vote as well as the buying power, and through the use of their vote and their dollar they can effect change if they want to. Secondly, it will be primarily the middle class which will suffer first and most from the change in life style and the trend of downward mobility taking place within United States society.[18]

Grindel's remarks make clear why the memories and the hopes that call house churches into existence in our land are dangerous for us, for we cannot but become ourselves the primary subjects of such a call to conversion.

In the United States, we middle class are the primary, though not exclusive group, of people whose story The Story calls into question. *We* are put at risk. This is not an inward turning self-concern, however. Because of the interdependence of systems, fundamental changes in our own story contribute to the social reconstruction of our American story. The system that our house churches care to reconstruct is the same system which oppresses both in our land and in many third-world areas. In systems, changes anywhere make changes everywhere. Because there is a world economic system, and because of the pervasive presence of the American socio-economic structure in that megastructure, what the church might elicit through imaginative fidelity to a middle-class mission in our country is awesome. But we should never for a moment underestimate the resistances deep within us to anything that even remotely feels like downward mobility. Dangerous indeed!

Why pay that price? Proximately, so that we may enjoy the freedom of release from our addictions. Even amid such affluence we are usually so at pain to know what to do with our leisure that we create new addictions to fill the time — television being perhaps the severest of American addictions. There is nothing that nurtures our consumerism as fiercely and effectively as television advertising.

But ultimately, and more importantly, we pay the price in order to cooperate with God in building up God's People so that all the children of God may wipe the tears from their eyes and sit at a table of fine foods and clear wines. The constant and celebrative reappropriation of that hope gives us the heart to live with dangerous memories. Eucharist is the key ritual celebration of dangerously liberating memories and hopes. It is a privileged moment in which the past, through both dangerous and consoling memories, and the future, through hope-full anticipation, collude in the social reconstruction of life upon the face of the earth.

The Discipline of the House Church

Throughout this book we have used almost interchangeably basic Christian community, small Christian community, intentional Christian community, and house church. In the final chapter of *Toward a Christian Economic Ethic*, Dan Finn and Prentiss Pemberton treat what they call "small disciplined communities."[19] This is another way of naming such groups.

Through their development of the adjective "disciplined" they have clarified further some of the key characterisics of the house church. What they mean by "discipline" also underscores the difficulty of creating this kind of community in our culture, because it means that we share power with others for the co-creation of ourselves. If *Habits of the Heart* is right, the surrender of autonomy is against the American grain with a fury and a fierceness. Giving other people power in our lives exposes the illusion of autonomous selves. Our condition is no less true just because ontological individualism is a distortion. For Americans perceive such individualism as true, and thus it becomes the sociopsychological reality out of which we live.

Finn and Pemberton address both community (inner workings in their definition) and action (their word for mission, or secondary group commitments). They mean communities that have at least four to five members, and usually not more than 15 to 20. In so far as such a group wants to begin to live in some new ways, they allow those new ways to become the norms of their house church's mini-subculture. They then expect one another to live according to these norms. And they give permission to each other to hold them accountable for so living. For there can be no community without both commitment and accountability. Neither can there be community unless some norms are co-owned and co-operative. That means that each person says in effect to every other person: "I agree to give you permission to call me to become what we have said we want to become. There are things you can expect from me and you can hold me accountable for them. When you do, you help me become what I want to become. And I agree to call you to become what we have said we want to become, and I will hold you accountable." These are not legal rules and regulations but the conditions of empowerment proper to a community. They are a covenant we make with one another:

Anyone who is not willing to allow a group to define at least *some* behaviors (e.g., time of meetings, procedures at meetings) has no real reason for joining any group. In

> fact, in nearly all groups that are of any importance to their members, patterns of expected behavior predominate . . . In a small disciplined community . . . the group members are critically conscious of the patterns of action expected. They self consciously discuss just what they will expect of one another . . . The most difficult thing for most people is getting used to the idea of belonging to a group that so self-consciously sets out to define what its external expectations will be.[20]

As we have repeatedly insisted, a house church's covenant covers not only its shared life within community, but its commitment to shared action in our larger world, that is, our conduct as a mediating structure within history.

To state it in secular terms, effective pressure groups are well organized. The People of God deserve no less. In mystical politicization, the religious experience and its social consequences for God's children both deserve equal asceticism and discipline. In this context, "organized" is another way of saying "disciplined." In the quest for racial justice and in the peace movement, groups were well organized both internally and in their corporate witness. They were effective precisely because of their organization. The change of social structure is gradual and difficult. The power of individual groups and networks of groups to facilitate social change reflects the level of discipline/discipleship they have been able to muster. Jesus took his disciples apart from time to time. The disciples then went out into the field and practiced what they had been taught. They returned to share their experience and receive critical feedback from their Rabbi. Sometimes they learned they hadn't prayed well enough! The disciples were a small disciplined community which attracted a following. Had they not had this attraction as a community, Rome would not have feared Jesus enough to pressure the collaboration of Caiphas the High Priest to remove Jesus from the scene.[21] A single man or woman *without followers* is not much of a threat to a society.

House Church: A Locus of Practical Theology

True theology is a present-tense verb and not a noun. It is what people of faith are doing *now* to locate their everyday lives within an ultimate context. Doing theology is one of the most important ways in which people of faith make meaning. Theology, therefore, participates in the social construction of the stories which a faith community "writes" in the world. It helps communities *make history*.

Theological reflection is one of the characteristic activities of intentional Christian communities. It is not, of course, the only kind of theology. Local theologies should in turn be primary grist for the mills of systematic theology in the academy, which has a vital role to play in integrating the broader experience of Christian church. But that is not our focus here.

We do not yet have a really good name for the new form that theology is taking shape in our culture. [22] "Praxis" and "practical theology" are technical terms that are sometimes used. But in popular usage in American culture, neither word is able to evoke the intrinsic connection between disciplined reflection and disciplined action. In traditional theology, the social setting in which a theology is forged does not make a self-conscious appearance in theological formulations. Liberation theology has a very different sound — it bristles with the particularity of local churches in their socio-cultural situation.

God's Word is an existential address to us in our immediate situation. It is not words on a page. For until the words of the text accost us, they are not yet the living Word. When they do accost us, it can only be in the immediacies of our lived experience. That makes crucial the careful conversation between our present situation and the Great Story. Social analysis is one of the most useful ways of interpreting the present moment. The abundance of contemporary historical biblical scholarship facilitates our more accurate interpretation of the Great Story, as it is instanced in the scriptures and tradition. Members of intentional Christian communities must draw on both kinds of interpretive resources.

We are stressing here the word *interpretation*. We never have bald, objective facts about anything. As we noted in Chapter Three, every fact is an interpreted fact. Many of the tools of social analysis are means of helping the present situation speak accurately for itself, and of interpreting what justice requires. What a particular situation needs now in order to be more just has dual effects: it guides the disciplined expectations that house church members have of each other in the lifestyle they share, and also the community's expectations about shared action in the world.

One does not, of course, have to be an expert in a field of social analysis to make a correlation between the present moment and the New Testament. Holland and Henriot stress the necessity of community members being inserted in the situations which they address. The expert in social analysis, therefore, may need to do a lot of listening to the experience of concretely involved Christians for basic information. Immediate raw experience is vital. On the other hand, however, when the present situation is as immensely complex as our socioeconomic system, insight from scholarly disciplines is both a critical theological tool and a movement of prayer as it rubs shoulders with the Word of God. House churches, therefore, must be concretely engaged in the systems to which they proclaim the Good News. And whenever expertise in social analysis can help clarify that engagement, it should be welcomed as an integral part of that church's faith life. It is a piece of *diakonia* to know well any situation to which we would offer a ministry of service.

If there is no uninterpreted present fact, equally there is no uninterpreted past fact. Each piece of the scriptures is a particular community's interpretation of sacred events. We have learned well that uncovering the historical Jesus is a tricky and deceptive undertaking since we cannot arrive at an uninterpreted Jesus. All our scriptures are records of how communities were effected by the Jesus event and remembered it through its effects on their particular lives. Each Gospel is an interpretation of the fact of Jesus. One of the aims of biblical interpretation is to identify how an ancient community's experience colored the Story as presented in scripture, and to free the Story as much as possible to speak with its own voice to the present moment. Here too we must say that not only biblical scholars have sensitive access to the Word on its own ground. Christians who have spent time in careful conversation with the Word have some instincts about it that study alone might never generate.

A community is doing practical theology when its interpretative analysis of its present situation enters into serious conversation with interpretations of its Great Story, and when that conversation points Christians into their Story's future.[23] Practical theology, then, is not an academic discipline that one explores for clues about what to do. It is a faith activity. As often as not, its setting is the liturgy of the Word. A community brings its accumulated experience into the liturgy and opens its experience up to the Word. Conversely, it also brings the Word into its experience and opens the Word to its lives. And it always asks: "So what?" Decisions follow for both a community's internal life and its constructive presence in history.

The Christian Great Story makes clear the priority of distributive justice over all other forms of justice. This is not a chronological priority, of course, because all justice bears upon all life all the time. But as far as values are concerned, until our most fundamental needs for a decent life are met, we are simply not available to the greater demands of history-making. When social analysis names consumerism as a middle-class behavior that sustains a system which in turn creates serious problems for social justice,[24] the members of a house church can begin to identify and choose specific non-consumerist behaviors. These behaviors can then become part of the community's covenant. And when enough communities share the same covenant in the world, the world's systems are affected. Fifteen years ago enough people refused to consume grapes and iceberg lettuce from California, and things changed.

Neither too much nor too little should be made of the role of expertise in social analysis and biblical interpretation. Not too much, because sensitive Christian people, whether educated or not, can engage in the conversation between the Word of faith and the exigencies of daily life. Not too little, especially in a middle-class situation, for there is no sense in wasting energy and resources when expertise is available or can be developed to give God's Word clearer and more practical direction in history.

The Possibility of Downward Mobility

While not all Christians in the United States are middle-class people, our culture is largely determined by middle-class mores. As we have indicated, even those who are not middle class are deeply affected by our social situation. We repeat that there is room and need for more than one kind of house church in our land, but we have focused on the house church in the setting of the American middle class. With Grindel, we are convinced that the church's mission to the poor is addressed both by immediate attention to the needs of the poor and to the social systems that keep them poor. It is in respect to the latter that we are recommending the efficacy of the house church in U.S. culture.

Every social system has a set of values out of which it lives. Upward mobility is a very important middle-class value for Americans. Consumerism is a principal behavioral tendency that expresses and supports this relentless upward appetite: we always want "better things for better living." We cannot reconstruct this socioeconomic system without taking consumerism head-on.

There are indeed very positive values in our socioeconomic system, such as the abundance it has been able to produce and the leisure time it has made available. We wonder how the system can be transformed so as to do two things: produce good outcomes and end poverty. We recognize that our memory of Jesus who brings Good News to the poor and sets captives free is dangerous to our consumer habits. It will cost us personally in our lifestyle if we try to build a future that is loyal to this dangerous memory of Jesus' promise to the poor. The cost will almost certainly include some measure of downward mobility, freely undertaken for the love of all our sisters and brothers, children of God. Some Duppies (downward urban people) will replace some Yuppies (the young urban professionals). The symbolic structure of our middle-class system give no support to doing with less. To change our system's symbolic structure so that it would at least tolerate and perhaps even reward Duppies would be a far-reaching transformation of the American story. However, nothing less than a fundamental reconstruction of our own socioeconomic system can ameliorate the problematic socioeconomic system of the rest of the world. Reconstruction does not, of course, imply replacement (nor does it exclude it). If we don't change our story, historical forces *outside us* are likely to change it. It is difficult to avoid the judgment that the recent growth in terrorism outside our country is often a desperate response to massive injustices, in some of which we participate, and that the increase in aggressive militarism within our country is a counter-response. Violence responding to violence is never a solution to violence. Addressing the injustice that spawns the violence stands a better chance.

The role of mediating structures in social reconstruction is essential. The house churches, the intentional Christian communities, are one such possible agent of reconstruction in our culture. Because of their voluntary nature, they can be one of the most effective means of evangelizing culture. Little systems can better affect big systems than individuals can. Networks of little systems are even more insistent conversation partners with megastructures.

We have also tried to make clear our conviction that the fundamental religious experience of Jesus out of which our Great Story originates is a story about relationships: with-God-with-one-another. Relationships constitute social systems. Politics is one inevitable dimension of how systems get on with it. Economics is another. Our immediate experience of God immediately politicizes us in our relational web.

In this chapter, we have dwelt upon some aspects of the world story and our American story. We might have focused on defense policies and nuclear disarmament, or upon the emancipation of women in Western culture and in the church. If we had, we would have made a similar case for the importance of house churches among middle-class Christian people in this country. On these issues too they can have clout. The Equal Rights Amendment will get passed when the middle class is sufficiently conscientized. Note that we have never suggested becoming only a middle-class network of house churches. House churches of every ilk are needed and they must network together. But we are strongly encouraging the American church not to forsake a critical mission to the middle class, because of the power that can be marshalled there for the good of the People of God. Such house churches can help create counter-subcultures which, because they have not withdrawn from their larger environing culture, can seep transformatively into the interstices of our American story.

Some of the memories we must kindle are "dangerous" to the middle-class lifestyles we enjoy. House churches are a home for dangerous memories and the transformative hope that such memories inexorably engender.

Affection for History

God made the world and God loves the world. Our Great Story is patently clear about that. The affection of God for human history could not be clearer. If there is a divine anger (and there is), it is reserved for those who prevent the earth from nurturing and loving its daughters and sons. Even that anger springs from a tenderness essential to the holiness of God.

Being holy like God means tenderness for historical experience, as God is tender. God's strategy for the good of the world is a redemptive Word addressed to individuals, of course, but also and overwhelmingly to a people. God makes Israel his people, and Israel itself is God's Word within and to history. Christians believe that in Jesus God also calls a People into life. This People too is God's Word within and to the world. It is the vocation of this People to make the Kingdom come in the structures of historical existence. There is no way to be a people or to work with the structures of history except through uses of power for the sake of good. Use of power means politics. At the level of concept it is a neutral word that names a fact of life. But in the world of events, politics constructs good things or bad things, never neutral things. One cannot be of the People of God, then, and be apolitical.

Some of God's people put their corporate lives together in house churches. In the more traditional sense of the word "mediate," house churches mediate the experience of God. In a second sense, they are *political* mediating structures which, in the context of our situation, elicit the social reconstruction of our American story.

Because house churches are social structures, they require leadership. The nature of a group always determines the nature of its leadership. That is the topic of our final chapter.

Additional Resources

Practical Theology

Liberation theology is the most developed form of practical theology. For a very competent discussion of these issues by an American theologian, we strongly recommend Matthew L. Lamb, "Liberation Theology and Social Justice," *Process Studies*, 14/2, 1985, pp. 102-123. Especially powerful are Lamb's reflections on the five -isms threatening human history: classism, racism, ethnocentrism, technocentrism and militarism. There are interrelated issues of the overarching issue of social justice. For a fuller discussion, cf. Lamb's *Solidarity with Victims* (N.Y.: Crossroad, 1982).

We have frequently referred to practical theology in this chapter. While there is much to learn from liberation theology, the socio-cultural setting of the so-called first world requires that we develop our own methodology and reflect out of our own situation, for which Johannes Metz's work is particularly helpful. *Followers of Christ: Perspectives on Religious Life* (N. Y.: Paulist, 1978) is a series of conferences given to the Association of Religious Superiors in Germany. In two short chapters Metz presents the mystical/political connection that is so central to his work. Cf. II/1 "The Christological Status of Following Christ," and II/2 "The Structure of Following Christ." It is worth noting that this political message is being addressed to members of religious communities — politics is not the preserve of the laity. *Faith in History and Society* (N.Y.: Crossroad, 1980), comes from the same period (1977 in its German publication). On practical theology, cf., esp. chapter 4 "The Concept of a Political Theology as a Practical Fundamental Theology." For both the title of this book and much inspiration, we call attention to chapter 5 "The Dangerous Memory of the Freedom of Jesus Christ. The Presence of the Church in Society." *The Emergent Church* (N.Y.: Crossroad, 1981), is a good example of local ecclesiology, although "local" in this instance is not the particularity of a smaller country, but the region of the Western first world. Metz's analysis of the bourgeois society and the bourgeois church is as pertinent to America as to Germany (which is his proximate concern). Cf. esp. chapter 5 "Christianity and Politics: Beyond Bourgeois Religion," and chapter 6 "Transforming a Dependent People: Toward a Basic-Community Church."

Local Ecclesiology

You can think of the universal church as broken down into various local churches or as built up out of those same local churches. In the first instance, local ecclesiologies become regional applications of universal ecclesiology. In the second instance, theological reflection arises first out of the faith experience of local communities, and universal ecclesiology is forged out of the many particulars. The whole is always more than the sum of its parts, and that is true of the universal church: it is a reality more complex and inclusive than local churches, and a fuller incarnation of the mystery of Christ. But this does not discredit the existential priority of local churches and local ecclesiologies, i.e., the basic ecclesial units. For a more generalized treatment of the need for and richness of regional theology, cf. Robert J. Schreiter, *Constructing Local Theologies* (Mary-knoll: Orbis, 1985). Relevant to the topic of this book, Schreiter observes that "the role of the community in developing theology reminds us also for whom theology is, in the first instance intended: the community itself to enhance its own self-understanding" (p. 16).

Local American Theology

Two Catholic theologians on the American scene who have been attending diligently to practical theology in our context are Matthew Lamb and David Tracy. Lamb's work has already been cited. We also call attention to David Tracy, "The Foundations of Practical Theology," in Don S. Browning (ed.), *Practical Theology* (N.Y.: Harper, 1983), pp/ 61-82. This essay is a characterizes practical theology and locates it within the larger theological conversation. In a similar vein, Schillebeeckx notes that a major task for academic theology is to assimilate local theology into the larger church's memory.

We already cited Dennis P. McCann and Charles Strain, *Polity and Praxis: A Program for American Practical Theology* (Minneapolis: Winston, 1985). We are also convinced that the empirical wing of process theology is one of the better American bets for a truly indigenous American theology. The process tradition, however, has failed to engage itself deeply in the particular issues of American culture. This is a key issued that William Dean addresses in *American Religious Empiricism* (N.Y.: SUNY Press, 1986).

Notes

1. Our religious experience is regularly mediated by and expressed in metaphor. We get our religious metaphors by ransacking the images and ideas that our culture makes available. "Father" is a metaphor for God that reflects cultural naming. It is a root metaphor for Jesus' experience of his relationship with God. In some ways God is like a father (care), and in some ways not (does not sire children). "Like" and "not like" are part of every metaphor. As our culture fights it way through non-inclusive langauge, it searches for an alternative for God as father. God as mother is a corrective, but is as one-sided as father, unless the two are regularly mentioned together. God as parent is more neutral, but parent does not conjure up the nurture and care that both mother and father are able to suggest. Even though parent is emotionally cooler than mother and father, it does partial duty as a metaphor: it tells us that because of who God is with and for us, the ultimate truth about us is that we are equals as sisters and brothers. To violate that equality between us is to violate God. Because king is a male figure, "Kingdom of God" has the same patriarchal bias. In this book we have tried to use People of God most of the time. But this, too is an ambiguous solution, because Kingdom of God evokes a Christian hope with immediate recognition.

2. Johannes B. Metz, *Followers of Christ: Perspectives on Religious Life* (N.Y.: Paulist, 1978), p. 42.

3. Cf. H. Wheeler Robinson, *Corporate Personality in Ancient Israel* (Philadelphia: Fortress, 1964). Because we are so thoroughly socialized in the notion of the autonomous individual as the basic reality (as Bellah makes so clear in *Habits of the Heart*), our tendency is to read the emphasis upon corporateness in other cultures as a primitive perception that needs to be corrected. However, it is impossible to hear Jesus' teaching on its own grounds without Israel's experience of corporateness as backdrop — or to hear Paul's profound sense of all Christians as one body without his Jewish education (as a Pharisee) as a backdrop. We are emphasizing the social nature of reality. We acknowledge the reality of the individual person, but reckoning with it as an emergent from relationships. Individuals do not first exist and then relate. Relationality is their truth from the beginning. Robinson's two essays are useful meditations on a way of being in the world that is rather foreign to American cultural instincts, but makes way for retrieving a corrective instinct.

4. Delbert R. Hillers, *Covenant: The History of a Biblical Idea* (Baltimore: Johns Hopkins, 1969), p. 51.

5. The New Testament itself is a very pluralistic document. There are multiple interpretations of what it means for Jesus to be named "the Christ." These different interpretations reflect different metaphors: Son of Man, Son of David, eschatological Prophet, Spirit Christology, Wisdom Christology, Logos Christology, etc. Interestingly, the title "Son of God" has a quite different meaning in the synoptic tradition (emphasizes a *human figure* chosen for a divine work) than in the Johannine tradition (emphasizes a *divine figure* chosen for a human work).

As Christian doctrine developed in a very Hellenized context, the Logos christ-ological tradition rather successfully pre-empted the other possibilities. Logos theology is preoccupied with questions about the nature of Jesus' relationship to the Father, and the nature, status and interrelationship of Father, Son and Spirit. The apologist and patristic traditions, as well as the great early Councils, are almost without reference to the parables and teaching of Jesus, to his life and work in Galilee and Judea. Consequently, in our inherited christological in-stincts, we have had to justify the attention we pay to our own relationships in community and to our obligations to the social structures in which we live., In a word, we have had to justify our affection for history, and have hardly even timidly claimed political concern as an *essential* christological issue.

6. Sallie McFague, *Metaphorical Theology: Models of God in Religious Language* (Philadelphia: Fortress, 1982), esp. Jesus as a Parable of God, pp. 42-55.

7. "Statistical Abstract of the U.S.A., 1986, p. 459.

8. Thomas E. Clarke, "To Make Peace, Evangelize Culture," *America*, June 2, 1984, p. 413. Emphasis added.

9. Dennis P. McCann and Charles R. Strain, *Polity and Praxis: A Program for American Practical Theology* (Minneapolis: Winston, 1985), pp. 8, 9.

10. Johannes B. Metz, *The Emergent Church* (N.Y.: Crossroad, 1981), esp. chapter 5.

11. Metz's analysis is in terms of the bourgeois — a term he admits is loaded. Bourgeois is not simply convertable into "middle class," but we have opted for speaking about our "middle-class" character because it might help make the point more easily. Bourgeois names not only an economic class but an entire set of values and behaviors. But its quite pejorative connotation makes it hard to recognize some of the positive achievements of the middle-class structure.

12. Metz, 1981, pp. 68-69.

13. Metz, 1981, p. 69.

14. Leonard C. Lewin, *Report from Iron Mountain on the Possibility and De-sirability of Peace* (N.Y.: Dial Press), p. 18. A purported report upon a think-tank commission to play peace-games, the work is generally recognized as fiction. However, its analysis of the nature of war-based economics and war-based structures of civilization is compelling. For support for Lewin's position, cf. Kenneth Boulding's "The World War Industry as an Economic Industry," in Emile Benoit and Kenneth Boulding (editors), *Disarmament and the Economy* (N.Y.: Harper, 1963). What becomes increasingly clear is the intimate connection between the bishops' pastorals on peace and economics. We hope they will increasingly articulate that connection. It will make a stronger case for both issues.

15. John Kavanaugh, *Folling Christ in a consumer Society: The Spirituality of Cultural Resistence* (Maryknoll: Orbis, 1984), p. 19.

16. Joe Holland and Peter Henriot, *Social Analysis: Linking Faith and Analysis,* (Maryknoll: Orbis, 1983); cited above in n. 15, Kavanaugh's *Following Christ in a Consumer Society: The Spirituality of Cultural Resistance;* Prentice Pemberton and Daniel Rush Finn, *Toward a Christian Social Ethic: Stewardship and Social Power* (Minneapolis: Winston, 1985); and the pastoral letter of the American bishops on Economics.

17.Kavanaugh, 1984, p. 27.

18. John A. Grindel, "The Church in the United States as Prophet," in David Fleming (ed.), *Religious Life at the Crossroads* (N.Y. Paulist, 1985), p. 104, emphasis added. the emergence of a new local sense of being church is evoking strong regional responses to the church's mission as it is particularized within concrete socio-cultural settings. Grindel's short essay is a very convincing presentation of the church as a middle-class institution with a middle-class mission. This is not to say that the church has no mission to the very poor or the very rich, but that the socio-cultural context for that mission to the poor or the rich is still that of a middle-class culture.

19. Pemberton/Finn, 1985, chapter 9, "Empowerment through Small Disciplined Communities."

20. Pemberton/Finn, 1985, pp. 212-213, passim.

21. Recent scholarship on the "why?" of Jesus' crucifixion is very important for several reasons. First, given the bitter anti-Semitism that has characterized so much Christian history, this recent scholarship offers a necessary corrective. It seems very unlikely that Jews would have had a motive for the execution of Jesus. Jesus' polemic with the Pharisees, for example, is in great part a retrojection of the polemic of the post-70 communities during the Christian split from Judaism. The teaching of Jesus is basically not at variance with that of the Pharisees. But the Romans would have had ample reason for getting Jesus out of the way, and Caiphas, the high priest, was an appointed pawn of Rome and not a religious leader selected by Jews for Jews (his vestments were kept under lock and key by the Roman procurator). On this issue, cf. Ellis Rivkin, *What Crucified Jesus?* (Nashville: Abingdon, 1984). The second issue of importance for this scholarship is that it underscores a socio-political nervousness as Jesus proclaims who God his Father is, and what the consequences are for the total context of human existence. This is a prime example of the twofold composition of mysticism and politics.

22. More and more attention is being paid in the context of American culture to the requirements of an indigenous theology. Currently one of the best sustained discussions is Dennis R. McCann and Charles Strain, *Polity and Praxis: A Program for American Practical Theology* (Minneapolis: Winston, 1985).

23. Our understanding of the activity of a house church in its liturgy of the Word or its theological reflection is similar to what David Tracy describes as practical theology in "Chapter 4, The Foundations of Practical Theology," in Don Browning (ed.), *Practical Theology* (N.Y.: Harper, 1983), pp. 61-81. Tracy observes that "theology is the discipline that articulates mutually critical correlations between the meaning and truth of an interpretation of the Christian fact and the meaning and truth of an interpretation of the contemporary situation" (p. 62). We have been stressing the critique that the Christian story might bring to bear upon the cultural story. It is equally the case that secular culture offers needed critical reflection to religion.

24. Kavanaugh, 1984, esp. Chapter 3, "The Commodity Form: Consuming and Marketing."

Chapter 7

SERVANT LEADERSHIP IN INTENTIONAL CHRISTIAN COMMUNITIES: THE EXERCISE OF RELATIONAL POWER

In the preceding chapters we have explored a possibility with you. One of its names is intentional Christian community. As a diverse array of such communities continues to spring up around the world, including budding U.S. versions, the Christian vision of humankind as one body is being rekindled. A worldwide web of small Christian communities is truly "reinventing the church" in our time.[1]

There is no such thing as an enduring group without leadership of some kind, and no such thing as vital intentional communities without dynamic leadership. The statement of Latin American bishops at Medellin in 1968 recognizes the necessity of adequate community leadership in the assertion that: "The essential element for the existence of Christian base communities are their leaders or directors."[2] The dangerously liberating memories and transformative hopes of small Christian communities will come to fruition in history and society only if such communities nurture the processes of leadership always present among them, and do so in specific, and in certain crucial respects countercultural, ways. And so we end our jour-

177

ney together by examining styles of leadership appropriate within intentional Christian communities.

Leadership in Communities: Delicate Balancing

Groups cannot be reduced to the sum of their parts. They have an order, a pattern, which cannot be accounted for solely as a function of the personalities or behaviors of individual group members.[3] For example, biologists studying the migratory patterns of animal herds may sometimes focus attention on a particular animal, but more often will keep a larger focus on the herd as a whole. The overall movement of a herd is always influencing, and being influenced by, the movement of individual members of the herd. Neither perspective is more valid than the other; each simply yields different information.

In recent times sociologists and social psychologists have come to understand leadership as a process within all kinds of lasting social groupings. This view, which is often associated with the systems orientation which we explored in Chapter Four, stands largely but not totally in contrast to a conception of leadership as a matter of individual traits, skills or knowledge. From this perspective, leadership involves a pattern of reciprocal influence and initiative that will inevitably emerge in some form as the concrete life of any social group unfolds.

When leadership is understood as a process which emerges within particular social contexts, it follows that the different types of social settings within which leadership is occurring inevitably call forth different forms of leadership. Such contextual differences — e.g., families vs. bureaucratic institutions vs. communities — are crucial with respect to what kind of leading is appropriate within them.

Every human group evolves structures, rules and methods for carrying out its particular tasks. For example, in families members typically share much more of themselves in both breadth and depth than would be appropriate within bureaucracies. In bureaucracies, participants are more focused on specific, well-defined tasks than is ordinarily the case within families. In families, rules usually emerge in mainly implicit ways from culture and the familial histories of parents; bureaucracies routinely make use of explicit rules, norms and procedures. In bureaucracies, the scope of participant obligation is specifically defined by a contract or job description; in families, our obligations to each other are much more diffuse.[4]

So leading well in a family means facilitating the capacity of family members to share themselves broadly and deeply and to encourage and acknowledge such personal disclosure by family members; to take part appropriately in whatever needs doing at a particular juncture in the family's life; continually to uncover and transform destructive or constricting family rules and expectations; and to care and be involved in one another's lives over the long haul in a fairly open-ended way. Family leaders can rely on power, control and reinforcement to achieve such ends only to a very limited extent; leaders promote genuine mutuality within a family not merely by overseeing or reinforcing or teaching it, but by engaging in it.

Leading well in a bureaucracy requires that the leader keep her or his revelation of self within appropriate limits and encourage others to do so as well; oversee the planning, integration, implementation and evaluation of specific tasks; develop appropriate and explicit rules, norms and procedures for the efficient functioning of the system; and see that persons are rewarded adequately for performing their specific tasks well. Bureaucratic leaders have significant means at their disposal for influencing the behavior of their subordinates; a core aspect of the logic of such systems is that monetary rewards, promotions and security are routinely tied to performance.

Leading well within family systems obviously means something quite different from leading well within bureaucratic systems. And while the kinds of differences we've named are not black and white (for example, family members often have specific tasks which are related to specific outcomes; a degree of mutuality matters in bureaucracies), they do illustrate important and pervasive differences in patterns of reciprocal initiative and influence within different settings. Families and bureaucracies are not the same kind of social animal! Their differences make a difference for leadership processes within them.

What about community leadership? Small communities are intricate social forms. We have repeatedly noted that such groups are hybrids of two other kinds of social setting: an intentional community is "kind of like" a family and "kind of like" a bureaucracy; it blends the characteristics of each.[5] Relations among community members tend to be more personal than in bureaucracies, but less personal than in families. Some task or mission is more important in communities than in families, but less central than in bureaucracies. Community rules and expectations are ordinarily far less explicit than in bureaucracies, but more explicit than in families. And so on.

Leading well within small communities means paying attention to the web of relationships which is a community and letting no task damage that web. Leadership in such communities must encourage and assist in organizing members to identify and pursue important community goals. And it must do both of these things with little if any of the "power over" their followers which characterizes typical bureaucratic structures.

Leadership within intentional Christian communities is primarily a matter of facilitating a collaborative, democratic process among community members. In such a process, many voices must be given a hearing, differences acknowledged, common interests identified within inevitable diversity, and courses of action chosen which as far as possible genuinely reflect a consensus of concerns among those involved. The hallmark of authentic communal leadership is the capacity to promote a unity which is respectful of the diversity of gifts present among us.

There is no one way in which an intentional Christian community must live in fidelity with its dangerously liberating memory; there are always multiple routes which could be travelled creatively. In the life of an intentional Christian community, how our routes are chosen and traversed is as important as what lies at their end. There are, as we have seen, a number of tasks to be undertaken in intentional Christian communities beyond merely having decent, mutual relationships. Many important matters have to be taken care of adequately if these basic ecclesial communities are to survive and thrive.

It is as inappropriate to refer to community leaders as "managers" as it would be to label them "parents." The unique challenge of leadership within small communities has to do with keeping the proper balance between management and mutuality in a social setting wherein the relationships are as important as any task to be undertaken. Families can fall down a bit on the task dimension of group life and still be good families. Within limits, bureaucracies can be (and typically are) stronger on task than on relationship issues and still be successful. Community is the social form in which tasks and community relationships must be kept in the most dynamic equilibrium. Leadership within intentional Christian communities must tend that difficult balance competently and faithfully.

Requirements for Effective Community Leadership

Community leadership must include adequate resources for the *task* side of community life. By that we mean the working knowledge and skills required for effective planning, implementation and evaluation in the particular context of small communities. And it must also be capable of nurturing the *relational* dimension of community life.[6] This requires adequate working knowledge and skills in the areas of fostering mutual relationships, attending to communal history and values, building consensus and dealing constructively with conflict.

Leadership training for bureaucratic settings is necessarily different from such training for community settings, largely because the working knowledge and skills a good manager needs are readily transferrable from one large organization or corporation to another. Thus training programs for bureaucratic leaders need not focus much on the particular bureaucracy from which the manager to be trained is coming and to which he or she will return, because the logic of bureaucratic systems is such that the knowledge and skills required for their management are fairly generic.

Such is not the case with community leadership. The particular history and character of particular communities must be taken into account if one intends to nurture the process called leadership within them now and for the future. Unlike professional managers, emerging community leaders are not professionals with a transferable set of competencies. Most of them are thoroughly local leaders, who are unlikely to move on to leadership roles in other localities. They are women and men who have assumed positions of community leadership largely because others within their communities respond to them as leaders and acknowledge them as such. Their leadership roles are granted to them by their followers, not mandated by institutional power and structure. They have emerged as leaders within particular communities. We must not lose sight of the fact that leadership processes within intentional Christian communites are a profoundly personal and local matter.

The early churches were attentive to the issue of demonstrated, functioning leadership as a condition for ordination. We have already indicated that leadership is not a set of personal qualities, but a kind of interaction that helps a community get where it wants to go. You are only *certain* of leadership when you experience it happening. The legitimation of already functioning leadership through ordination is a way of saying that leadership forms follow leadership functions.

Although eucharist both causes and expresses community, it is properly celebrated only by an already constituted Christian community. That means that community presidency precedes eucharistic presidency. The Christian scriptures state clearly that communities celebrate eucharist. But there is no un-equivocal evidence in scripture or the documents of early Christian history about who presided at eucharist. There is a fairly broad conclusion among contemporary scholars, however, that whoever presided in community presided at eucharist.[7] During Vatican II's work on *Lumen Gentium*, the Central Theological Commission prepared background texts for section 28, twice mentioning that "in the primitive churches priests presided at the eucharist because they presided over the Christian community."[8] Although most Christians remember the Council of Chalcedon for its christological formulations, Canon 6 from that council is also fascinating. It not only forbids the ordination of a priest or bishop who does not have a specific tie to a specific community, but says that if such an ordination occurs, it is invalid.

Although there is simply not enough information available to warrant unambiguous generalizations about the practice of the early church in this matter, we can still be rather certain that it was typically the communities themselves who proposed candidates for ordination, and that the persons proposed were those who were already effective community leaders. This is the converse of present practice, as was already indicated in Chapter Two: instead of ordaining someone for eucharist and then sending that person to lead a community, the early Christians probably ordained an already-functioning community leader who then presided at the community's eucharist.

The memory of the early church in this regard is a dangerous one for currently established practice in several ways. If the earlier model worked its way back into ecclesial practice, not simply to be replicated, but strongly to condition current practice, the community's voice in leadership selection would have to be coordinated with the hierarchy's voice. Power would be at stake. Also, in those instances where the actual leaders of communities are women, they would become natural candidates for ordination in our cultural circumstances.

Let us not suppose that these memories would only be felt as dangerous by members of the hierarchy, because power issues would be touched so deeply there. Although they are often (and sadly) reluctant to speak loudly about the issue, many clerics are supportive of women's ordination. There is, for example, a national organization called "Priests for Equality." If not all clerics are opposed to rethinking our current leadership structures, neither are all lay women and men in favor of doing so. Or, to put it differently, our memories of communal and eucharistic leadership practices in the ancient tradition are potentially dangerous in some measure to the entire ecclesial system in which all Christians participate.

These memories of our early communal history feel like a gift in and for our time. For creatures of memory and expectation like ourselves, more ample alternative futures inevitably spring from more adequately retrieved pasts. It is our contention that the nearly forgotten past which we have been discussing here is particularly valuable today because it instances a paradigm for community leadership which has genuine kinship with what the contemporary social sciences are commending to our attention.[9] While the acknowledgement and legitimation of natural, actual, demonstrated leadership is crucial within the new house churches, it is good for church everywhere!

Let's now look more closely at the specific character of leadership within intentional Christian communities.

Community Leadership: Diverse Tasks, Different Gifts

We have seen that authentic intentional Christian communities are identifiable on the basis of four fundamental activities that take place within and emerge from them. Such communities are concretely committed to building up genuinely mutual relations between and among their members, engaging their history and society knowingly and actively, and standing in solidarity with other communities, individuals and groups with similar commitments. And they are committed to these three things precisely because the dangerous memories embedded and transmitted in the Christian narrative clearly call for them to take up that stance in the world. To the extent that intentional Christian communities are true ecclesial units of *koinonia, diakonia* and *leitourgia* formed in the central images of the Christian *kerygma*, leadership within them will have a necessarily diverse character. In order to underscore this crucial point, we will look at each dimension in turn.

First, every intentional Christian community requires leadership in building mutual relations. There must be those among us who cannot only model the basic skills of mutual interaction, but support and challenge others to engage in them as well. At a deeper level, there must be those among us who have dealt and continue to deal with their personal version of the transferential ghosts which can distort human relationships, and break up the community's body. Special gifts for leadership in building up and sustaining *koinonia* and *diakonia* among community members are not given to everyone.

Second, every intentional Christian community requires leadership in cultural and social awareness and engagement. There must be those among us with strong concerns in this area who can help our communities build the basic working knowledge and skills to be faithful to this dimension of our communal commitment. Interaction with those who have actually been engaged in the struggle for racial and sexual equality, for social and economic justice for all persons, is critical for vital leadership in small communities. Special gifts for leadership in building up and sustaining a community's *diakonia* in human history and society are not given to everyone.

Third, every intentional Christian community requires leadership in establishing connections and pursuing joint efforts with other communities, movements and individuals who share values compatible with the community's. There must be those among us who are capable of helping our community not only to preach but also to practice solidarity by means of deliberate and effective networking. Such persons understand the delicacy and discipline of communicating, planning and sharing resources among groups with diverse histories and agendas. Special gifts for leadership in building up and sustaining inter-community *koinonia* and *diakonia* in society and history are not given to everyone.

Finally, every intentional Christian community requires leadership in maintaining vital links between its practices of *koinonia* and *diakonia*, its ritual celebration or *leitourgia*, and the *kerygma* whose narrative carries forward the dangerously liberating memories and expectations of Christian tradition from generation to generation. There must be those among us who can assist us in maintaining an authentic conversation with our sacred texts. There must also be those among us who can draw us together in sacramental moments, moments wherein our common deep story and vision are given potent ritual expression. Such communal practices of word and sacrament continually deepen and purify the community's long-run efforts at mutuality, social engagement, and solidarity with others, by locating the everyday commitments of community life within the ultimate context of the Christian *kerygma*. Special gifts for leadership in building up and sustaining nurturing and challenging communal conversation with and ritual celebration of the Christian story and vision are not given to everyone.

If gifts for leadership in any of the four areas of life in intentional Christian community are not given to everyone, it is even less likely that gifts for leadership in all four areas would be given to anyone. Once we have properly understood the four essential and interrelated dimensions of life within such communities, it becomes evident that leadership within them cannot be adequately carried out by one designated leader. At her or his best, the designated leader is one who will recognize, evoke, nurture, celebrate and help to unify the manifold gifts residing in an intentional Christian community for leadership in all of the areas just described.[10] As this process unfolds, community members are affirmed in their gifts and challenged to develop them. This is how gifts multiply among us.

Having established the necessarily diverse character of leadership within intentional Christian communities, let's turn our attention first to our most common cultural conception of leadership, and then to an unsettling — and profoundly Christian — alternative.

Leadership as Relational Power

In the vocabulary of contemporary U.S. citizens, "leadership" is intimately associated with words like "influence," "direction," "initiative," "control," "authority," "power," and so on. If, as we have seen, a people's language not only describes but shapes the world they live in, then our culture's synonyms for leadership tell us something important about our commonly held understandings and assumptions regarding leadership among us. What they tell us, in essence, is that we take it for granted that leadership is primarily a matter of having effects of a certain kind on others. But how adequate is this conception?

Leading and following require each other. They are terms of relationship. The notion of a leader with no one following is no less absurd than that of a follower with no one leading. Leadership and followership are interrelated aspects of the same relational dance. Leading entails a delicate balance of having and receiving effects, of receptivity and initiative, of influencing and being influenced. But our common cultural vocabulary of leadership words (and likewise our common conception of leading) does not include "being influenced," "receptivity," "empathy," "being affected," and so on.

We have seen that intentional Christian communities are dialogical communities of equals; mutuality and inclusiveness are their hallmark. There can, therefore, be no place for unilateral leadership — leadership as initiative and influence flowing only in one direction — within them. This does not mean that the leader is to refrain from initiative and influence within intentional Christian communities. What is required rather, is a re-conception of leadership among us, one that takes adequate account of the receptive dimension of being a leader.

The classic statement of influence among us as a reciprocal event, a matter of having *and* receiving effects, is Bernard Loomer's magnificent essay entitled "Two Conceptions of Power."[11] Loomer defines "relational power" as "the ability both to produce and to undergo an effect," "to influence others and to be influenced by others."[12] He asserts that "the conception of relational power, in contrast to power conceived as unilateral, has as one of its premises the notion that the capacity to absorb an influence is as truly a mark of power as is the strength involved in exerting an influence."[13] In the practice of relational power among us, we acknowledge the reciprocal character of all human relationships. This is not to say that effects in relationships are necessarily or even typically balanced or symmetrical; often they are not. It is to insist, however, that relationships are inevitably reciprocal; effects are felt on both sides, from both sides.

Loomer's insistence on the reciprocal character of our relationships is not merely a description of what he takes to be the facts, but also an invitation to recognize that the relational practice of power expresses a particular value. He writes:

> Our readiness to take account of the feelings and values of another is a way of including the other within our world of meaning and concern. At its best, receiving is not unresponsive passivity; it is an active openness. Our reception of another indicates that we are or may become large enough to make room for another within ourselves. Our openness to be influenced by another, without losing our identity or sense of self-dependence, is not only an acknowledgement and affirmation of the other as an end rather than a means to an end. It is also a measure of our

own strength and size, even and especially when this influence of the other helps to effect a creative transformation of ourselves and our world. The strength of our security may well mean that we do not fear the other, that the other is not an overpowering threat to our own sense of worth.

The world of the individual who can be influenced by another without losing his or her identity or freedom is larger than the world of the individual who fears being influenced. The former can include ranges and depths of complexity and contrast to a degree that is not possible for the latter. The stature of the individual who can let another exist in his or her own creative freedom is larger than the size of the individual who insists that others must conform to his or her own purposes and understandings.[14]

Loomer's point is clear: the capacity to be transformed by another's presence and effects is as profoundly a sign of personal strength as the capacity to influence another.

Let our point be equally clear: the creative practice of leadership within intentional Christian communities does not entail a refusal to exercise initiative and influence, but rather a commitment to be responsive to the initiatives and influences of others while also having one's own effects. In the gospels we are told explicitly that lording it over others — the unilateral use of authority — is not to happen among us. Creative leadership within Christian communities involves the practice of reciprocal influence as a relational event. Our ultimate warrant for this assertion is to be found in the classic images of leadership from Christian scripture. Let us now remember those dangerously liberating images.

"As One Who Serves"

We indicated in the previous chapter our conviction that the teaching of Jesus upends many of our most accustomed and most basic structures of relationship. The nature of leadership among us is one such structure. Authentic leadership within Christian communites can only involve initiative and influence among equals. The followers of Jesus form a discipleship of equals. Jesus teaches us the shape of the Kingdom; he is rabbi, not us:

> But you are not to be called rabbi, since you have only one master, and you are all brothers and sisters. You must call no one on earth your father, for you have only one father, and he is in heaven. Nor must you allow your-selves to be called teachers; you have only one teacher and he is the Christ. The greatest one among you must be the servant. (Mt. 23: 8-11)

The key to the vision of Jesus is that the parenthood of God makes all of us sisters and brothers. God's parenthood puts an end to human patriarchy. As Elisabeth Schüssler Fiorenza indi-cates, God's parenthood may not be used to support patriarchy because it functions "precisely to reject all such claims, powers, and structures."[15] God's parenthood is "a critical subversion of all structures of domination."[16] Once again it is clear how inti-mately related are the mystical and the political dimensions of our lives. Because of who God is for us, and therefore who we are called to be to one another, domination is not a legitimate option in the exercise of power among us. It is not surprising, then, to see the attention which the Gospels give to the nature of leader-ship within a discipleship of equals.

Mark's Gospel recounts an argument on the road to Jerusalem, which for Mark is the road to the cross. James and John ask Jesus for a privileged place at his side in glory. The other ten followers are indignant with them. Jesus says to them:

> As you know, among the pagans their so-called rulers lord it over them, and their great men make sure their au-thority is felt. You must not let this happen among you. Rather, anyone who wants to become great among you

must first be a servant, and anyone who wants to be first among you must be a slave to all the others. For the Son of Man did not come to be served but to serve . . . (Mk 10:42-45)

In Mark's Gospel, the disciples usually have a difficult time understanding what Jesus is really saying (the women in Mark are more understanding and responsive). Matthew rescues the silly disciples by having the mother of James and John do their silliness and ask for privileged places for her sons. Jesus' reply is the same.

A significant change takes place in Luke's Gospel. The argument about greatness occurs at the table of the Lord's Supper, after the account of eucharistic institution. Jesus repeats the answer he gave in Mark and Matthew, but adds a meal metaphor:

For who is greater, the one who is at table or the one who serves [the table]. The one at table, of course! But here I am among you as one serves. (Lk 22:27)

Here is the upending of structures again. It is surely a theological reason that inclines Luke to takes this particular discussion off the road to Jerusalem and relocate it at the Last Supper. What could give a clearer message to a community celebrating eucharist than to hear this discussion about leadership take place within the very context of Jesus' institution of the eucharist?

John's Gospel does not recount the furor occasioned by the request of James and John. However, he narrates a dramatic washing of the feet at the Last Supper. Jesus doesn't just say, "as we have moved around and lived together, you must have noticed my behaviors with you — they were never unilateral. You, therefore, should do likewise." He acts out the servant's role, actually washing the feet of his community's members, a slave's task. The message about the function of power in the Christian community could not be stronger!

Leaders who serve receive effects as well as having them. Servant leadership is the Christian *kerygma's* name for leadership as relational power. When we practice the servant form of leadership in our communal life, we locate the everyday acts of initiating and responding among us within the ultimate context of Christian memories and expectations. We are among our sisters and brothers "as one who serves." But what specific, everyday acts embody servant leadership — leadership as relational power — within intentional Christian communities?

Relational Power in Community Leadership: Concrete Illustrations

In "Leadership and Power," Evelyn Eaton Whitehead draws on contemporary psychological studies of small group development to identify four recurring issues in the life of all groups: inclusion, power, intimacy and effectiveness.[17] While all four issues are always present in the life of a group, they tend to come into focus at different times, and often in a somewhat predictable sequence. "The best image perhaps," she writes, "is one of shifting priorities: at different moments in our life together as a group, different questions come to 'center stage' and demand more of our time and energy."[18] The life of an intentional Christian community will predictably involve cycling and recycling through times of primary concern with these four issues. Let's look briefly at each of the four basic tasks of group life and at the exercise of servant leadership (i.e., leadership as relational power) in each case.

Inclusion

Inclusion is the task of group life that involves members coming to be a part of a group's interaction, to feel as if they belong. In the absence of an adequate sense of being included on the part of at least most of its members, a group will not be able to muster the collective energy necessary to fulfill its mission.

Servant leadership in the formative stage of an intentional

Christian community takes the form of hospitality, of personally welcoming members to the newly forming group. There are no more profound ways of including someone in the life of an intentional community than by inviting them to tell their stories and then acknowledging the contributions that are forthcoming. It is no less important that leaders share their own stories and hopes for the community's life, thereby identifying themselves as partners in an incipient dialogical community of equals.

Another way of indicating that servant leadership fosters inclusion by eliciting the telling of stories and sharing of gifts is to say that an important way of facilitating a sense of belonging among persons is by providing a simple structure to help a community "get going." The literature on small group dynamics demonstrates clearly that such a structure can support and integrate a group while its own inner cohesion has the opportunity to develop.[19] Authentic servant leadership, of course, requires that these beginning structures of inclusion be in the service of the group building up its own identity and agenda, rather than promoting the leader's unilateral agenda. Potential community members will be quite sensitive to which of these approaches is actually operating.

While belonging is inevitably a focal issue in the beginning of an intentional Christian community, inclusion issues arise from time to time throughout the life of any group. The skills of mutuality discussed in Chapter Five are obviously critical for servant leadership whenever inclusion is the group's current priority.

Power

Power is the task of group life in which members learn to engage in mutual influence in a creative, reciprocal fashion. The issue here is how a group enables its members to exercise their different gifts appropriately and potently in the service of the group's mission. Groups always function as more or less than the sum of their individual members. A group's power or influence will similarly be more or less than the individual powers of its members, depending on the kind of leadership resources it can mobilize.

Servant leadership in the area of power is particularly crucial, because, as we noted in Chapter Five, issues of leadership and authority are breeding grounds for transference. When an intentional Christian community is relatively comfortable as regards inclusion, it becomes highly likely that a kind of contest of influence will emerge in some form. When it does, whoever had been exercising a leadership role is likely to experience a challenge. It is important to observe that these contests and challenges vary in their quality and intensity, from bitter and hostile attacks to assertive and mature proposals of alternative courses of action for the community's life.

Whitehead reminds us that, far from simply being negative events, this development signals a growth in group maturity. She also notes that leaders need not be passive victims of attacks during these inevitable attempts to balance power among us. She writes:

> The designated leader is usually in a position of some considerable power when the first questioning of leadership occurs. If the leader uses that power against the group member who questions, the rest of the group learns that new patterns of power will not be easily won. The message is given that the stakes are high in the process of change. If, however, the designated leader does not respond to this question as if it were a personal attack, a different tale is told. The message here is that power in the group need not be interpreted as a personal possession and jealously guarded from attack. Rather it is a resource of the group that needs to—and can—be examined, accounted for, and even redistributed among us.[20]

Authentic servant leadership in intentional Christian communities means embracing and fostering the mutual, reciprocal practice of influence and initiative — the practice of relational power — among community members.

Intimacy

Intimacy is the task of group life which involves negotiating an adequate and appropriate degree of personal closeness among members. Because an intentional Christian community has some of the characteristics of a family and some of formal organizations, it must find a level of personal sharing which is suitable to its goals and fits with the needs and preferences of its particular members.

Within some intentional Christian communities, the sharing of feelings and dreams and the willingness to work on relationships between and among members will tend in a deeply personal direction. Membership in such communities may be a primary source of emotional support and challenge, of companionship and intimacy, in the lives of their members. Or cordial, supportive, but less personally involving relationships may obtain in a community, with members finding their primary intimacy connections elsewhere. As long as an adequate degree of mutuality is present within a community, either of these options, or any point between the two, offers perfectly legitimate resolutions of the issue of intimacy. It is also not uncommon for communities to find that their intimacy norms and behaviors go through significant changes over time, changes that must be worked out in ongoing negotiation.

Servant leadership in the area of intimacy involves assisting a community to recognize that differences are likely to exist in members' hopes and fears regarding closeness among them, and to negotiate those differences directly, respectfully and with an appropriate measure of flexibility. At a deeper level, leadership in this area calls for an awareness of how transference creates barriers to intimacy in all human relationships, as well as a sense of when these barriers can be appropriately worked on within the group and when outside help is required for individual members or the entire community. Because of the intensely personal character of intimacy questions and the strong feelings they tend to generate in all of us, servant leadership on this issue will put the mutuality skills and commitments of community leaders to the test in a unique way.

Effectiveness

Effectiveness is the task of group life which involves movement from mission to goals to action to evaluation. In these moments of a group's life, Whitehead writes, "its chief priorities now are clarity about its task and the effective use of its resources to meet this goal."[21] If the three basic tasks of intentional Christian communities are mutual relationships, social awareness and engagement and networking, then the effectiveness of such communities has to do precisely with the quality of their sustained efforts along those three lines.

Servant leadership in the area of effectiveness is a matter of nurturing the community's sense of mission and vision, fostering community consensus about particular goals, coordinating and stewarding the resources of the community in pursuing its chosen agenda, assisting the community realistically to evaluate its effectiveness, and keeping the results of such evaluation in conversation with the community's mission and vision. Such leadership requires many of the kinds of working knowledge and skills which professional managers in our society use every day; what is different, of course, is the ultimate context within which leaders of intentional Christian communities locate their concern for community effectiveness.[22] Authentic Christian communities are never concerned with effectiveness for its own sake or for the sake of profitability; they are always concerned with their effectiveness in inserting the dangerous memories and transformative hopes embedded in the Christian narratives into their history and society.

We have already insisted that gifts for community leadership in building mutual relationships, nurturing an informed and deliberate engagement with history and society, networking with others of similar purpose, and guiding community practices of word and sacrament are given to various community members. Similarly, gifts for community leadership in the areas of inclusion, power, intimacy and effectiveness do not belong to the designated leaders, but reside in the community as a whole.

Servant Leadership and Creative Transformation

Leonardo Boff has written that:

. . . in a certain sense it is unrealistic to struggle for a 'classless society' — a society that would be simply and totally a community of brothers and sisters, without any conflict at all. Realistically one can only struggle for a type of sociability in which love will be less difficult, and where power and participation will have better distribution. Community must be understood as a spirit to be created, as an inspiration to bend one's constant efforts to overcome barriers between persons and to generate a relationship of solidarity and reciprocity.[23]

Our firm conviction is that the formation and networking of small intentional Christian communities in the U.S. portends a significant contribution to the transformation of history and society so that "love will be less difficult." The dangerous memories and transformative hopes of Christian tradition are of human beings standing in solidarity and reciprocity before their God. As persons within intentional Christian communities learn to exercise our influence and initiative relationally, to become leaders who serve one another and the world, to redistribute power and participation among us, to make a unity of our multiply gifted diversity, barriers are overcome and the ancient Christian memories and hopes are rebirthed in and for our time.

Additional Resources

Leadership

The theory of "situational leadership" is presented by Paul Hersey and Kenneth H. Blanchard in *Management of Organization Behavior* (Englewood Cliffs: Prentice-Hall, 1982, fourth edition). This approach to leadership builds on a distinction between "task" and "relationship" dimensions of group life, one that parallels the distinction between the primary-group and formal-organization dimensions of community life.

Gerard Egan's *Change Agent Skills* (Monterey: Brooks/Cole, 1985) is written for persons in helping and human service professions such as counseling, social work, education and ministry, who find themselves called upon to intervene in systems of various kinds. It contains many practical models applicable to both task and relationship dimensions of life in intentional Christian communities, including an excellent chapter on leadership.

Leadership in the Christian Community

In *Ecclesiogenesis: The Base Communities Reinvent the Church* (Maryknoll: Orbis, 1986. Translated by Robert R. Barr) readers will find a highly readable account of the role of the *communidades de base* in the transformation of the Latin American church. Generalizing from that experience, Boff argues powerfully for the necessity of mutually creative transformation between small, local ecclesial units and the institutional hierarchy of the Catholic church. Especially thought-provoking from the perspective of leadership in intentional Christian communities are his treatments of the lay leader and the celebration of eucharist, and the possibilities of women's priesthood.

Michael A. Cowan (ed.), *Ministerial Leadership in Community* (Collegeville: Liturgical Press, 1987). This volume, which is one of a series on sacramental experience in our time and culture, is the fruit of an interdisciplinary conversation among sacramental theologians, social scientists and liturgists on the subject of emerging forms of ministry and leadership in the Christian church. It contains contributions by James Whitehead, David Power, Evelyn Whitehead ("Leadership and Power," the essay referred to extensively in this chapter), and John Shea. Also included are a set of rites which embody a relational conception of ministerial leadership as power and service within a dialogical community of equals.

David N. Power examines the possibilities of lay ministry in the Catholic church in historical and theological perspective in *Gifts That Differ* (N.Y.: Pueblo, 1980). Power offers rites for the recognition of various lay ministries including vigilance and hospitality, word and worship, and mutual hospitality.

Edward Schillebeeckx's new and expanded theology of ministry is to be found in *The Church with a Human Face* (N.Y.: Crossroad, 1985. Translated by John Bowden). This is a richly grounded historical exploration of ministry in the Catholic church. Schillebeeckx's treatment of authority and leadership call adult Christians to a full measure of baptismal presence in and responsibility for their church. It is a definitive account of the authentic meaning of Christian ministry, a truly precious resource for the members of contemporary intentional Christian communities.

In James D. and Evelyn Eaton Whitehead, *The Emerging Laity: Returning Leadership to the Community of Faith* (N.Y.: Doubleday, 1986) readers will find a challenging account of power and authority in the American Catholic church as interactions within community life, rather than possessions of designated institutional leaders. They examine the proper place of such power and authority in Christian life, in dealing with such topics as the exile of leadership, the crisis in ministry, the recovery of charism and conscience, and the discernment of idols and prophets.

Servant Leadership

Robert K. Greenleaf's *Servant Leadership* (N.Y.: Paulist, 1977) is a series of meditations in essay form by an experienced consultant in the field of management. They are remarkable for their employment of the servant metaphor to illuminate authentic leadership in a variety of settings including business, education, foundations and churches.

Relational Power

Perhaps the classic account of power as relational is Bernard M. Loomer's "Two Conceptions of Power," *Process Studies*, 6/1 (1976), pp. 5-32. In this essay, which is deeply informed by the process/relational metaphysics of Alfred North Whitehead, Loomer offers a radical reflection on and critique of the one-sidedness of our traditional understanding of power as unilateral. At the core of Loomer's presentation is an exposition of "The Constitutive Role of Relationships" (pp. 19-21), in which the co-creative character of human relationships is examined. Of particular interest to members of intentional Christian communities is Loomer's challenge to an understanding of "unilateral love" in the Christian tradition, an understanding which he sees as a fundamental distortion of the relational character of genuine love.

In *Poets, Prophets and Pragmatists: Challenges of Pluralism to Religious Life* (in press), Evelyn M. Woodward offers an analysis of community life replete with theological reflection and discussion which will enrich the life of any intentional community of faith. Woodward's treatment of "Transfigured Power in Community" (chap. 6) is a remarkably fruitful translation of and practical meditation on Loomer's "Two Conceptions of Power." Her reflections on community (chap. 2), and on empathy (chap. 3) and conflict (chap. 4) in community relationships are full of wisdom and a deep and seasoned pastoral awareness.

Notes

1. The phrase "reinvention of the church," is often heard in the context of the Latin American *communidades de base.* Its ecclesiological implications are powerfully displayed in Leonardo Boff, *Ecclesiogenesis: The Base Communities Reinvent the Church* (Maryknoll: Orbis, 1986. Translated by Robert R. Barr).

2. Cf. Medellin document on "Joint Pastoral Planning" in volume two of Louis Michael Colonnese (ed.), *The Church in the Present-Day Transformation of Latin America in the Light of the Council* (Washington, D.C.: United States Catholic Conference, 1968-69), pp. 10-11. Cited in Boff, 1986, p. 15.

3. On groups as organisms with a life of their own and leadership as a process of reciprocal influence among persons within all kinds of social groupings, cf. Evelyn Eaton Whitehead, "Leadership and Power," in Michael A. Cowan (ed.), *Ministerial Leadership in Community* (Collegeville: Liturgical Press, 1987).

4. On the character of primary groups in contrast to formal associations, cf. Evelyn Eaton and James D. Whitehead, *Community of Faith* (N.Y.: Seabury, 1982), chap. 3.

5. On the character of communities as hybrid or intermediate social forms, cf. Whitehead and Whitehead, 1982, pp. 25-32.

6. On the "task" and "relationship" dimensions of any group's life and a "situational" approach to leadership style based on that distinction, cf. Paul Hersey and Kenneth H. Blanchard. *Management of Organization Behavior* (Englewood Cliffs: Prentice-Hall, 1982, fourth edition.); and Gerard Egan, *Change Agent Skills* (Monterey: Brooks/Cole, 1985), pp. 205-207.

7. Cf. Herve-Marie Legrand, "The Presidency of the Eucharist According to the ancient Tradition," *Worship*, 53/5 (1979), pp. 413-438; and Schillebeeckx, *The Church with a Human Face: A New and Expanded Theology of Ministry* (N.Y.: Crossroad, 1985. Translated by John Bowden).

8. Legrand, 1979, p. 413.

9. Cowan (ed.), 1987.

10. On the acknowledgement and celebration of multiple gifts in Christian communities, cf. David N. Power, *Gifts That Differ* (New York: Pueblo, 1980).

11. Bernard M. Loomer, "Two Conceptions of Power," *Process Studies*, 6/1 (1976), pp. 5-32.

12. Loomer, 1976, p. 17.

13. Loomer, 1976, p. 17.

14. Loomer, 1976, p. 18.

15. Elisabeth Schüssler Fiorenza, *In Memory of Her* (N.Y.: Crossroad, 1983), p. 150.

16. Schüssler Fiorenza, 1983, p. 151.

17. Whitehead, 1987, pp. 43-55.

18. Whitehead, 1987, p. 44.

19. Cf. Richard L. Bednar and Theodore J. Kaul, "Experiential Group Research: Current Perspectives," in Sol L. Garfield and Allen E. Bergin (eds.), *Handbook of Psychotherapy and Behavior Change* (N.Y.: Wiley, 1985, third edition.)

20. Whitehead, 1987, p. 51.

21. Whitehead, 1987, p. 52.

22. For a practical primer on the working knowledge and skills necessary for change agents, which are also quite important for effective leadership, cf. Egan, 1985.

23. Boff, 1986, p. 5.